SEXUALLY SHY
The Inhibited Woman's Guide To Good Sex

SEXUALLY SHY
The Inhibited Woman's Guide To Good Sex

Charlotte Kane

BUKOD BOOKS

For the lovers.

Published byBukod Books.

Paperback ISBN-13: 978-0-9840574-6-7
Paperback ISBN-10: 0-9840574-6-3

First published in the United Kingdom and the United States in 2006 by
New Tradition Books under the *title Good Sex: A Woman's Guide to
Losing Inhibition.*

eBook ISBN–13: 978-0-9840574-7-4
eBook ISBN–10: 0-9840574-7-1

CONTENTS

BETTER SEX

We all know the saying, "better than sex." Some people say that chocolate is better than sex. Others say that bungee jumping is better than sex. Still others claim that drugs are better than sex. Supposedly, there are a lot of things out there that are better than sex. However, I never use this saying because, to me, there *is* nothing better than good sex. And in my opinion, people who use this saying might not be having the best sex.

Isn't it time you did?

Sex to me is about getting off and doing whatever feels good, which, in turn, releases tension and makes life good. When the sex is good, everything is in tune, and everything is engaged—your soul and your heart and your body and just everything. You feel every single part of your body at once and there's nothing like it.

What's also great about good sex is that when you are having it regularly, life seems a little less heavy and a bit easier to deal with. Your problems are just problems and not the sum-total of who you are. This is why everyone loves sex; it just makes a person feel so good.

However, good sex isn't that easy to come by. If it were, we'd all be having it right now instead of reading books about having it. Things get in the way of good sex. For instance, we get stressed and push sex to the back of our minds. After all, sex rates low on the totem pole of important matters, doesn't it? It's not *that* important. It's not something we *have* to do. It's not something we *need*, right? It's just something we do from time to time that feels good and then we usually forget about it until next time.

But we don't really forget about it, do we? For many, it can be weeks or even months between sex. During those weeks or months, we start to feel funny, different. We start to wonder what's wrong with us, why we don't want it like we used to. Our inhibitions start to rear their ugly little heads and after a while sex becomes nothing more than a chore. Why bother? There's always something else we can do instead.

And that's what this book is about. It's about freeing yourself to get to that better sex and having that better sex. It's about overcoming inhibition, i.e. shyness, and getting past issues that might be hindering your sex life.

During the course of this book, I am going to talk about some things that usually aren't discussed. I believe the most inhibiting factors for most people with sex are repression and the distractions of everyday life and not lack of ideas or positions.

However, in addition to the talk of inhibition and repression, I am going to give suggestions about things you can do to rev your sex life up. Hopefully, this will be an instructional book for you. It might open a new door or two for sexual adventure, but then again, it might open your eyes as to why your sex life isn't where you want it to be.

One last thing, I am not going to spend time on sexual diseases and pregnancy. I assume you're an adult if you bought this book and most adults already know about this stuff. If you're one of the very few that doesn't, just know that you can contract diseases from sex—AIDS, etc... Also, women can get pregnant when they have sex. Always use a condom and/or some other form of birth control. This is important stuff, so be aware. And always be careful. And it's never a bad idea to get an AIDS test with or without your partner.

Keep in mind that I am just an ordinary person and not an "expert" and these are only my experiences and opinions. You do not have to replace your opinions for mine. What follows are just suggestions that you might choose to incorporate into your sex life. It's up to you what to do with the information. For me, sex has been an ongoing learning experience. I have learned how to enjoy it and lose my own inhibitions bit by bit. It's about the stuff that I needed to know and work through that no one ever told me about. These experiences are what I want to share.

In the end, it's not really about *how* you do it; it's just about doing it and having a good time *while* you're doing it. Once you can sort through the murk that muddles up your mind, you can get to the better sex that surely awaits you. And once you can do that, not only will your sex life improve, but your life as well.

PLEASE ALLOW ME TO INTRODUCE MYSELF

I am just an everyday, ordinary married person who wanted to write a book on how to be sexually confident. One of the reasons was because in my earlier days, I didn't have good sex. In fact, the sex was somewhat mediocre. And it wasn't anything my partner was doing or not doing; it was what I was doing or, rather, not doing. Sex never appealed to me in the way it appealed to the characters I had read about in trashy novels and it didn't make me weak in the knees. Sex was just sex and it was, at best, something I did a few times a month with my husband. I didn't look forward to it and I certainly didn't daydream about it. In fact, I just didn't care that much about sex, period. Moreover, if I could get out of it, I would. My shyness was overwhelming. How did I become this way?

I didn't know that things were about to change and they changed when I discovered sexual freedom. It was a gradual change but quite an effective one. And all it took was me confronting my issues and dealing with them. Once I did that, my mind opened up and this led me to be more sexually confident. Not only did I want to have sex with my husband more often, but I found that the sex was unbelievably hot. I finally understood what all the fuss was about. Sex was good! Sex was great! Sex was worth putting the effort into! It was so good, in fact, that I began to wonder if others had gone through what I had gone through and if they, perhaps, might benefit from my findings.

When I first began contemplating writing this book, I thought about the reasons why I should and how I had gotten to the point in my life that I am at now. I also wondered what I could accomplish with a book about good sex. One of the first things that popped into my head was the fact that none of the so-called good sex books out there ever touched on subjects that were hindrances in my own life. They never talked about the issues behind the lack of libido or the reasons why we need good sex books to begin with. They never really talked about having sexual confidence. It was all about the proverbial different position or the strawberry in the champagne. It was more about putting on a show than about digging deep.

I didn't want to do that. One reason why is because everyone has done that. I also thought that these books glossed over issues. They never seemed to get to the root causes of why we develop a lack of passion once we're in a relationship or, more importantly, why we never developed a passion for sex in the first place. Therefore, I wanted to write a book that would not only give suggestions to good sex, but help with underlying issues that are relevant but always seem to get overlooked.

That's when I came up with the gist of what would become this book. When I discuss the things that I do in this book, I'm coming from a very personal place as these are issues I've dealt with. For instance, when I was growing up, I had a very controlling mother who didn't teach me about sex but who taught me that sex was bad. After I got married, I found myself in a severe sexual slump and didn't know how or why I had gotten there. Not surprising, I've found that there are a lot of other people out there who have dealt with the same issues I've dealt with. It was only through years of personal introspection did I come to the conclusions that are in this book.

I hope this book will help you on a path of not only sexual freedom but also self discovery. I've found that it is only when we deal with our issues that we can overcome them. One way to deal is to bring them out into the open and confront them. Liberation only comes with recognizing that there might be something amiss and then dealing with it. And that leads to sexual freedom and, most importantly, sexually confidence.

SEXUAL BAGGAGE

There are many contributing factors to a lackadaisical sex life. The first could be distractions of everyday life. Another could be an over-abundance of stress, which can turn the most uninhibited person into a prude. Other factors could be health concerns or a new baby. Money issues, weight issues and family issues can all contribute to less sex and more worry. This leads to stress and inhibition. Everyone recognizes these issues as hindrances to a good sex life. However, one of the main overlooked issues is sexual baggage and, in some cases, it can be one of the most dominating factors that keep us from having good sex.

So what is sexual baggage? Sexual baggage is basically issues we haven't dealt with and that we've brought into our sexual relationships. Sexual baggage, basically, is our hang-ups and it can lead to a total lack of sexual confidence. It is usually set down once a person gets into the newness of a sexual relationship and then picked back up once the initial excitement of the relationship wears off. Therefore, it's always been there, it just gets pushed aside once a new relationship starts. I believe this is one reason many people tend to jump ship once the "new" wears off. They are terrified of confronting their sexual baggage and would rather roam from one relationship to another than deal with their issues.

However, not dealing with these issues is what can lead to a lack of sexual confidence. Upon confronting then, they usually tend to go away.

It's no secret that we all want better sex. This is why there are so many books on the market that explain how to do things "better." But what most of them leave out is the simple fact that, while new positions and toys can be exciting, it is what *we* bring to the bed that really matters. And, if what we bring has been tainted in any way, our sex lives start becoming acutely problematic and when this happens, we lose sexual confidence. When we bring sexual baggage to bed with us that usually means we're not going to enjoy sex. It's important to know that baggage can usually keep us from enjoying sex as it was meant to be enjoyed.

To me, sex has been too over-explained. There is too much discussion about positions and kinky sex but not enough talk about what keeps us from actually enjoying it. And most of us know that it's what's between our ears that count and not what's between our legs. Our genitals don't keep us from enjoying sex, our minds do.

Yes, "mechanically" we can get it together, but if our whole bodies—brains included—aren't engaged, why bother? It usually leaves us empty and sometimes feeling used. Usually, it's not about our partners, it's about us and our inability to deal with our issues. It's much easier to place blame than take responsibility. It's much easier not to look at why we lack sexual confidence than actually do something about it.

If you look back at your sex life, you might recognize a pattern. When you first met your lover, the sex was out of this world, wasn't it? In the beginning, you were a wild and free sexual creature, but now you're wondering what went wrong. As I've said, many things might have contributed to this, including the fact that you might have had some kids, gotten a more stressful job or perhaps you're experiencing problems with your family or a health crisis. There are many things that can contribute to a sluggish sex life. But, in my opinion, the main problem with it usually doesn't come from outside sources, but from what's going on inside your mind.

Sex loses its luster once the "new" wears off and then many of us tend to try and "fix" our relationships, rather than deal with what really and truly bothers us. Sex becomes the issue when the lack of desire is usually just covering something else up. Then we begin to wonder what went wrong and why we once enjoyed sex so much. That's because, in the beginning, it's easy to set the baggage aside. You've just met the love of your life, after all. Sex is exciting and it's fun! Who'd want to do anything else but have sex?

But once the "new" wears off, and you find yourself in a routine with your lover, the sex normally dies down a bit. This is nothing new and it happens to most couples. It's hard to keep that momentum up. In fact, after a while, it can be taxing to do it as much as you did when you first fell in love. As I said, this is normal and part of most people's lives. It's nothing to worry about. However, if you're not *ever* looking forward to having sex, then something else may be at play. And one of the biggest culprits is *sexual baggage*. When you enter into a new relationship, you have your baggage, but, like I said, you can set it aside in the beginning and enjoy what your lover has to offer. Nevertheless, after a while, the baggage comes back and it's only purpose is to mess your sex life up. Our baggage is usually our excuse not to enjoy sex. And this is where sexual confidence is usually lost.

We all have baggage and that's what I am going to discuss in the following chapters. The most important thing to understand is that once you deal with your baggage, you can usually leave it behind. It's then that it no longer bothers you. Sometimes just bringing the issues you have to the surface is enough to make them disappear. Not always, but sometimes this is possible. And, with that possibility, comes good sex and sexual confidence.

A SLUT IN THE BEDROOM

We women sometimes do this thing which I like to call *taming the inner slut*. We all have it in us to be these totally uninhibited sexual creatures but then something happens to scare us back into our shells, turning us into these shy little creatures. This is usually caused by those little voices that tell us to hold back and not get what we want. This is part of our sexual baggage.

One way to tame the inner slut is to take offense at being called one. If we're called one, that means we're acting like one and if we do that, we're bad. And, yes, sluts, generally, are seen as "bad." They sleep around, get diseases and steal other women's men using their womanly wiles. Being a slut is a bad thing. It's the kind of girl your mother raised you *not* to be. So, in an effort to be a "good" girl, we submit to taming the slut inside of us.

However, what we do is not only tame the slut in ourselves, but we kill her. We don't want to be seen like the proverbial bitch in heat. What would others think? While it is good to have control over our sex lives, it's not good to totally disown our sexuality and part of our sexuality includes the ability to behave like a slut.

By behaving like a slut, I don't mean that you have to sleep with thousands upon thousands of men or take your clothes off at any opportunity. What I mean is that you can be a good girl *and* be a nympho with your partner at the same time. All this entails is that you get over generalizations of words like "slut" and, once you can do that, you can stop allowing it to be detrimental to your sex life. In fact, when we succumb to these generalizations, we are allowing other people to control our behavior. All because we don't want anyone to think we're "like that."

Most men don't have to deal with this. It's almost funny to call a man a slut. But if you call a woman a slut, then she's no better than an animal, right? What we do when we bring our baggage into the bedroom is let words like slut take over our minds. We don't want to be seen as slutty in our everyday life, so it spills over into the bedroom. And this, in turn, leads to inhibition.

One way to describe the word slut is "a woman who likes sex a little too much." Is that a bad thing? Supposedly, it can be. Even in our culture today, being called a slut is seen as a bad thing. Sure, it's nice to see it acted out in a movie or on TV occasionally, but for most of us, this isn't a possibility in our lives. In effect, if we can't be sluts in our everyday lives, how can we enjoy sex at all?

The point is you can be a slut without ever leaving the house. You can be a slut for your lover. We can all be sluts. We just have to get over the idea that being a slut in the bedroom is a bad thing. And how do we become sluts in the bedroom? It's simple—*all we have to do is get into and start enjoying sex.* That's all a slut is. She's a woman who enjoys sex. At least, in my opinion, she is.

It's a known fact that most men, especially those who are open-minded, love women who love sex. And we all know most men love sex, period. But then most men weren't born trying to live down a word like "slut." This is mainly because ninety-nine percent of them have never been called one. Women are always under the threat of being called a slut and do have to live this word down. It's not a good thing to be called a slut, just as it's not a good thing to act like one.

If you can begin to recognize your inner slut, you will realize it's no big deal. All it entails is letting loose during the time you're having sex. It doesn't have to take all night, though if it goes into overtime, no one complains. Getting into sex is crucial. It's also what your lover wants you to do. He has to know he's turning you on and, if he doesn't care, he's a jerk. But I'd be willing to bet your man is a lot more interested in you having massive orgasms than you think. And I'd be willing to bet that he wants to assist you in achieving them. Just ask him.

But how to get to it? How do you engage your inner slut? First of all, you need to recognize that you have it in you. *Oh, no,* you say, *not me. I am not slut. I'm a good girl.* You might need to realize that when it comes to having sex with your significant other, the two terms are not mutually exclusive. A person can be a good girl in the real world and a slut in the bedroom all at the same time. In effect, once the bedroom door is closed, you can turn into a wild, sex-loving slut.

This is about *unleashing your inner slut.* And it's not that hard to understand. It's just the flip side of being inhibited. It's about allowing you inner slut to come out and play and, while you're at it, lose your inhibitions to get to that better sex. It's about getting rid of all the nonsense we've been fed for years about sexuality.

And how do we unleash our inner sluts? I think it all begins with admitting to ourselves that we like sex. Recognize your inner slut. Think about how good sex makes you feel. It satisfies you, right? It can be empowering as well. All you have to do to make it work for you is to take that attitude and mold it to benefit you. And let's face it. You're no prude. You wouldn't have picked up this book if you were. You've been sexually adventurous in the past but maybe you're in a slump or you just want to take that next level and really step up your sex life. Or maybe, sex has lost its luster for you and you don't understand why. Maybe you just want to be more sexually confident.

It's not all about having wild and crazy sex, though that is a big part of it. It's about giving yourself *permission* to have wild and crazy sex. It's about giving yourself permission to get what you want out of life and not feel guilty about it. It's about recognizing what you want out of life and not what someone else told you *should* want. It's yours, after all, isn't it? Isn't it about time to get what you want? By becoming a slut in the bedroom, you will start enjoying your sex life more and more. And you'll probably be one happy person.

If you don't like using the term "slut" to describe yourself, come up with another word that you do like. However, in the end, it's all the same. You might just want to be the kind of girl who loves sex and is willing to try just about anything. You might want to be the kind of girl who craves sex and is not afraid to flaunt her sexuality, sometimes explicitly. *Be the girl you want to be.* That's what having sexual confidence is all about.

It's all about having the right attitude. It's about not letting the world get you down. It's about taking bad life experiences along with the good. You want to be the kind of person who doesn't just live life, but who embraces it.

You can be sexually empowered and you don't have to apologize for it. Once we lose our sexual power, or disown it, it's all downhill from there. Own your sexuality. It's a force of your personality as much as your sense of humor, if not more. Everything about us is about sex, from the way our bodies are shaped to the way our emotions lead us. Sex is our life force and without it, the species will die out. It's that simple, it really is. Sex is a necessity as much as it is an enjoyment. Without sex, none of us would be here.

It's important to know that you have everything you need. You weren't shortchanged. You weren't born with "something" missing. All you have to do is bring out what is naturally there. You've got it all. Isn't it time to use it to your advantage and to start getting the most out of your sex life? Isn't it time to get some real sexual confidence?

MOTHER, MAY I?

Mother doesn't always know best, does she? Not in my case, anyway. I'm sure many of us can remember a time when, for whatever reason, our mothers taught us that sex was bad. That made us very confused, didn't it? I know it certainly confused me. I can remember having sex dreams and not knowing what was going on. I can remember thinking "dirty" thoughts but not knowing why I was thinking them but feeling bad because I was. I was so confused during that time I thought there was something wrong with me. I didn't know it was this thing called puberty.

And that's when my mother decided it was time to warp my thinking concerning sex. It was just so wrong and so dirty. I should never stoop to such a level. It was bad, dirty and totally disgusting. I was only about twelve when she started this, so, therefore, I was thoroughly confused about what she was talking about. However, the message I got was clear—sex was bad. But I didn't really know what sex was. I was totally naïve, a little sheltered and more than confused. If sex was bad, then fine, it was bad. But, please, tell me what sex is!

She never did. All my two sisters and I got were confused messages. All sex was bad, all the time. There was also this religious connotation to it, as well. I was taught that if I had sex, I'd more than likely burn in hell for it. It's a wonder I ever got over this.

One thing my mother told us that was totally contradictory was, "Boys don't get pregnant. Girls do. Don't get in trouble." Again, I was confused and my mind spun for days over this new bit of information. Sure, technically, boys don't get pregnant but don't they have *something* to do with it? I knew they did but what they did was still out of my grasp. I couldn't reason with it and, unfortunately, I didn't have anyone I could ask about it, either.

I would sit for hours and think about it. Girls got pregnant from having sex. Right? I knew boys were somehow connected to all of this, but how was beyond me. I didn't have Sex-Education to help, either. So, I went around for years wondering what it was all about and I think I was in my twenties before I even began to gauge how badly she messed me up.

Thanks, mom.

So, for me, I just detached myself from my sexuality and hoped I wouldn't get in trouble. Boys liked me but that wasn't good because if they *touched* me I might get knocked up. I didn't even know that a penis had to be inserted into a vagina in order to make a baby. As a result of this, I grew very inhibited. It took years to break out of that and to realize that it wasn't me that had the wrong idea about sex, it was my mother.

Okay, I suppose I could excuse her for all this and I do. And the reason I excuse her is because I know she was only trying to protect me, even if it was in this extremely warped way. I eventually came around because I realized that sex isn't wrong. It's the ideas other people put into your head that are wrong.

But it took a long time for me to get over the idea that sex was "bad." All because of what my mother had drilled into my head, perhaps to save me from the horrors of teen pregnancy. She made me feel dumb and insecure and weird about the whole thing. Regardless, I bought into what she was saying because, like most young girls, I wanted to please my mother. I didn't want to do anything to upset her. And that meant I had to disown my sexuality.

When I met my first boyfriend, I was one-hundred percent virgin. I'd never even been kissed by a boy before. It embarrassed me whenever he'd want to kiss because, truth be told, I didn't know how. Not only was I a seventeen year-old virgin, but I was a seventeen year old prude!

The only problem with that was the fact that I had fallen in love with him. And, when one's in love, things just naturally progress. However, when things went too far, I'd hold back and push him away. I didn't push him away just because of what my mom had told me, but also because I didn't want him to see me "down there." I was totally ashamed of myself, of my body and of my desires. I shouldn't be doing this stuff! It was bad! Yet, I wanted to do it, as any teenage girl in love wants to do it. But I could not let my guard down. After all, my mom was inside my head still and she was still telling me not to get in "trouble."

Fortunately, I had met a very persistent guy who not only didn't mind to wait, but didn't *care* to wait for me. I was lucky in the fact that he never pushed himself on me and that made me trust him and, as we all know, trust is the most important thing you can have in any relationship. And as our relationship progressed, so did our sexuality. Soon, we were having sex and it was the best thing in the world for me. Of course, I had the occasional thought about what a "bad" person I was, but I managed to put that aside long enough to have a good time.

It was only after I was married did the thoughts my mother had planted in my mind come back. And that's when the trouble in the sex department really started. I began to not want it. I kept putting it off, hoping my husband wouldn't notice. In fact, I became so inhibited that it would have been alright with me if we never had sex again. I didn't know why this was happening to me and to my relationship, but I knew I was responsible and for that I felt bad.

Thoughts would creep into my mind randomly: *Sex is bad stuff. I can't do it. I can't like it. What would that say about me?* With thoughts like these, I became very inhibited. Even though I liked sex and enjoyed doing it, I still had my mother in my brain telling me what I was doing was *wrong*. I had this unfounded fear that my mom would find out what I was doing and somehow punish me for it. It got so bad that one night I had a dream I was in bed with my husband, attempting to have sex, and suddenly my mom was in bed between us! Of course, she was giving me a very disapproving look and shaking her head. (Wouldn't Freud have a field day with this?)

In effect, my mother was controlling my sex life, not me.

Try as I may, I could not get her out of my head and that meant I couldn't enjoy sex. Sure, I had it occasionally and it was good most of the time, but I had a lot of guilt. I had this deep, instinctive feeling that there was something wrong with me. I felt shame for wanting to have sex and then I felt guilty for not giving it to my husband. This created a vicious cycle. Soon, I didn't care if we had it and tried to avoid it at all costs. What sexual confidence I had gained in the beginning of our relationship was completely diminished.

We all know that shame is projected from an outside source and I had that source—my mother. With shame, we feel that something is wrong with us and that leads to guilt. Shame and guilt are from the same family. When they happen, along comes repression and until you deal with it, you will always be repressed. I knew that in order to deal with my issues, I had to deal with the things my mother had taught me about sex.

I came to this conclusion one day when I was sitting around feeling miserable. I knew I was in a sexual slump. I thought about why I felt the way I did about sex. I was almost a prude and couldn't even allow my husband to look at a nudie magazine without blowing up at him. I couldn't watch porn because it was just so "disgusting." And I could never, ever masturbate. But I was tired of feeling this way, of being so inhibited. I was tired of worrying about what my husband was thinking all the time and I was sick of being frigid.

And then it dawned on me. I felt like this about sex because that's what I'd been taught growing up. It's like a lightbulb went off in my head. I was a grown woman. I didn't have to hold onto the same ideas I had when I was a kid. Sex wasn't bad or evil. Sex was good. Just because my mother had told me one thing didn't necessarily make it so.

That's when I decided I owned my body and I was my own woman and if wanted to masturbate or watch porn, I could. It had nothing to do with my mom anymore. All I had to do was stop believing the many untruths she'd told me. And so I did. I began to dismantle them one by one until one day, I was able to initiate sex with my husband and ask him to watch porn with me. I kept doing it little by little until the old associations were gone.

It was a long time in the making, but I did it, I released my mother's stranglehold on me. I did that by dealing with the inhibition and untangling myself from her issues. And just because she had issues with sex doesn't mean I have to.

Humans don't naturally dampen their sexuality. The trouble starts when they're taught to hush it, just like I was. Sexuality is in all of us and in everything we do. It's not going away and it never will, either, thank God. Think of all the books and movies and television shows that are all about sex. Look around you. I'll bet you'll see a million phallic symbols without even trying. (The Washington Monument comes to mind.) Just because someone tells us it's wrong—like my mother did—doesn't mean it is.

You have to, at some point, stop living your life for others and start living it for yourself. Just because my mother was wrong about sex does not mean I have to go around with a bag over my head ashamed and acutely aware of my sexuality at all times. Just because she disapproves of sex doesn't mean I have to.

We get so caught up in doing the right thing that we let it force every bit of joy out of our lives. It's not "right" to have sex and it's not "right" to be happy when other people are miserable. No, it's not right to teach children that what comes naturally and should be a source of unlimited happiness is wrong. That's not "right" and it will never be right. When someone does that, they do nothing but shame their victims into doing the "right" thing by making sex into this unforgivable and dirty act. Sex between two consenting adults is pure joy. There is nothing in the world like it.

But some of us just can't get over our hang-ups. We become stunted and unhappy. Stop here and ask yourself what good your unhappiness is doing for the world. Pain in our lives does not make everything all right, nor does it make us happy. Disowning our sexuality because of something a mother said does nothing but keep the guilt alive and happiness out of reach.

What I had to realize was that I was the owner of my body. I had to come to the conclusion that I was the one who held onto these beliefs when they'd long outlived their original purpose. And, quite frankly, their intention was to keep me from teen pregnancy. My mother was raising three girls and that worried her—a lot. I suppose the only way she could make sure we didn't sleep around and get knocked up was to plant these terrible untruths about sex into our brains.

It did take some time, but it was time well spent. It is a journey a person has to make if they really want to enjoy their sexuality and that's what sexuality is in us for—to enjoy. So, I say, do what you please as long as it's not hurting anyone else. You wanna get down and dirty? Hey, go out and get down and dirty. Do it in an alley next to a garbage can if you want to. Some people are looking for someone to give them permission to "do" it. Give yourself permission to do it. *You own your body!* It's yours to do with and what you damn well please. It belongs to you. You are responsible for feeding it and taking care of it, so why not own *all* of it? Own your vagina and your breasts just as you do your eyes or your ears. You can use it in any way that you want. Again, with feeling, *you own your body!*

But for some reason, it's just so hard to own ourselves, isn't it? We don't want all that responsibility that goes along with it. We want men to respect us—even the men we're married to—and the only way to do that is to keep our legs closed. We've been taught that if we have sex with a man, he automatically loses interest. You know what? That's *his* problem.

I have released my mother's hold on me. It does not mean I have cut her out of my life or anything like that, it simply means I am living my life for me. It means she doesn't dictate the terms of my sex life anymore. *I do.* Whenever I find that I am acting in a way I "should" instead of in a way I want to, I force myself to stop. It's hard. Her grip is strong, but it's not unbreakable.

In the end, I realized I had to drop the resentment against my mother or I'd never enjoy my sex life. More importantly, I had to accept that, in order for *me* to change, I had to allow *her* to change as well. This means that I couldn't keep looking at her as the main authoritative figure in my life. And, quite honestly, I think she was sick of that as well. I had to take responsibility for my life and this allowed her to let go, too. People do grow and they do change but, in order for this to happen, we have to let the past go and that means we have to allow others their own developmental growth and change. Sometimes stepping aside is the best thing we can do for each other.

And I prevailed. I realized that the poison my mother put in my mind was just a way to control me and my behavior. I realized that in order to be happy, good sex is a necessity. It is a stress relief and releases so many good endorphins. It takes the clouds away on a rainy day and it makes a person feel really alive. That is the best thing about sex—it's power to make you feel like someone.

And how on earth could that be a bad thing, mom?

REPRESSION

I think sexual repression is the root cause of a lot of misery in the world. Saying sex is bad is almost like cutting your nose off to spite your face. You are putting down the very act that put you here on this planet.

If we allow others to dictate our behavior, we become unhappy. Society and family tend to dictate our sexuality. However, we get all kinds of different messages about sex: It's good to like sex, just don't flaunt it. But if you do flaunt it, flaunt it the right way. *What?!*

Also, we're told if "you're going to act that way" then you should expect bad, terrible, hideous things to happen to you. And in what way are you acting? Usually you're flaunting your sexuality and when someone does that, bad things tend to follow. Or, at least that's what they tell us.

In our society we either reward sexual behavior, such as with our movie stars who can bed-hop like it's a spectator sport without condemnation; or we condemn it, such as we do when we find out someone at work cheated on someone else. It's okay if movie stars do it; they're "that" kind of people, but what was *she* thinking?

And, no, I am not condoning cheating, but, people, it does happen quite a bit. The point I am trying to get across is simple. We get mixed messages about sex and one of the most prevalent is: It's good for some but not for others. The other message is: It's bad and it causes a lot of unnecessary trouble. Sexuality is in all of us and it holds us together. We all want it and we all want to do it. But we just don't want anyone to put us down about wanting it.

The point of all this is that you need to overcome repression before you can be sexually liberated. Repression is poison in the minds of all people. Ask yourself why you're repressed and examine it and then let it go. It's as simple as that. I knew my repression came partly from my mother and partly from my society.

People are unnecessarily put into either of two classifications. Either you're sexual or you're not. You're a slut or a prude. You're a stud or a wimp. They leave out the middle ground but I'm here to tell you that there *is* a middle ground and that's where most of us live, without classification. We're just people who work and who have families and who have sex. Some of us are neither sluts nor wimps. We're just people. Yet, we put so much into what other people are doing and passing judgments on them that we don't even know what *we* like anymore.

Why should it matter so much who is sleeping with whom? What should it matter if you watch a little porn or masturbate to a picture of your favorite star? What should it matter? It shouldn't!

All of this "talk" keeps us from just doing it and from enjoying it. None of us want to be falsely classified or given a "bad" name. However, all this does is repress us. All this talk about who is doing who and doing what and about why it's so wrong. That's why, in my opinion, it's so important not to plant those bad seeds in heads about sex in the first place. And if we've had them planted in us, we need to weed them out.

One way is to start to recognize what's going on. When you're having a feeling of repression, ask yourself where it's coming from. If you can begin to sort all this out, you can set yourself free and not just sexually. And once you've tasted freedom, it's hard to go back into a prison.

Then there's this prevailing attitude that if you enjoy sex and/or have slept around, you're damaged goods and no one will want you. All the men in the world will see you as a big floozy and think you're no better than an animal. Even in today's "liberated" world, we still have to deal with issues like this. What's wrong with this picture? A woman who revels in her sexuality is seen as a loathsome creature. Women aren't supposed to enjoy sex, only men are. Women are supposed to be pure and without lust. In fact, we're supposed to virginal.

This whole idea of the virgin, the pure person who waits on her Prince Charming, is extremely juvenile. It's like you're supposed to sit around with your legs crossed acting like a proper young lady until Mr. Charming comes along and rescues you. The attitude is that there is no way he'd want you after you've been touched by another man. Also, women who think this way usually keep acting like this even after they've bagged Prince Charming. What good does this kind of thinking do anyone?

People, we're in the new millennium now. Why do we still have this attitude? Because society still dictates that women should be pure, even though we've all been sent these mixed messages. We see women on TV flaunting their sexuality and sleeping around but if we see someone else doing that in real life, we want to persecute them—just like in the old days. Have things really changed that much?

It's gotten so bad now that many women are claiming to be born-again virgins. Presumably so they land a good man. These women have had sex but decided that they're going to stay celibate from now on until they're married, thusly "reclaiming" their virginity. This is all well and good, but, really, why bother? What's happened has happened. If it was a mistake, accept it as such and get over it. A person can never erase his/her past sexual experiences. And why would anyone want to do that? It's best just to make peace and move on and grow from the experiences rather than disown them.

I believe if we would all start to own our sexuality and not let men or society or family dictate what we do, we could be much happier. This starts by accepting our past experiences and learning from them, which was the intention of having them in the first place. This starts by everyone getting over silly notions of "damaged goods." And once we can all do that, we can enjoy sex for what it is: Pure ecstasy shared between two people. And that's all sex is. It's ecstasy and it's fun. If we can get over the ideas that others have put into our minds, we can free ourselves to be the sexual creatures we are. We can free ourselves of our inhibitions and allow our sexual self to come out and play. We can become sexually confident. And, in the end, that's really all it's about.

PLEASE FORGIVE YOURSELF

All of us have things in our sexual pasts that we're not very proud of. Even though some of us still look back and beat ourselves up over it, we need to realize that what's in the past is in the past. If we don't, this kind of regret can lead to repression and repression, as we all know, leads to a dull sex life.

If you find that you are in this kind of situation, the only thing you can do is forgive yourself and move on. By doing this, you will free up some of that inhibition that is being caused by your self-contempt. Self-loathing is very counterproductive and a complete waste of time. No bit of sexual confidence can come from it.

As I've said, we all have things we'd like to erase. The best way to erase them is to forgive and forget. So what if you had a lot of one-night stands or you allowed some sort of behavior from a past lover that you wouldn't allow now? That's in the past and disowning it won't help things. However, allowing yourself to move through those emotions you've bottled up in an attempt to forget will get you over it.

None of us are perfect and we do all make mistakes. It doesn't really matter what you've done, all that matters is to forgive yourself for it. You might be blocking yourself from sexual pleasure in order to punish yourself. There's no need in this.

Guilt has a way of permeating us and choking the joy out of living. We have all lived with some form of guilt but we don't have to. We need to realize that everyone makes mistakes. One good way to overcome this is to sit down and write about it. Just take an hour or so and write down everything you feel, admit your mistakes to yourself, one by one and then, forgive yourself. Feel the emotions you're trying to cover up. Just feel what you feel as it comes. You might want to laugh, you may want to cry or even cringe in embarrassment and that's okay. Do it. And once you're done, you're done and you can move on to some amazing sex which will make your life so much better.

Always be cool with yourself. You're all you've got. Remember that and take this time to forgive yourself. This is an important step and shouldn't be overlooked. This will help build confidence not only in sexuality but in life, as well.

AN OPEN LINE OF COMMUNICATION

What is so important in any relationship, especially a sexual one, is an open line of communication. When you can be honest and not feel that anything you say will be held against you at a later time, sex not only gets better, it gets downright wonderful.

In my earlier relationships, I was mum about what I wanted. I thought that my lovers should instinctively know what to do to me, when and where and how. I didn't think I should have to speak up for myself and let him in on my inner workings. Well, I couldn't have if I'd wanted to because I didn't even know what pushed my buttons or even really turned me on. Later on, I knew what turned me on and what brought me to orgasm. I knew how to get what I wanted. But it was only after I shared this bit of information with my lover that I got it.

Unfortunately, I had been under the illusion that all men are born knowing every single little thing about sex. One reason might be because men are more curious about sex and more open to it than women. But if you think about it, men are *allowed* to be more open and curious about sex because for them, it's a different world they live in. They're not worried about getting pregnant or being called a slut, right? However, that doesn't mean they know everything about sex.

But we do think that, right? Most women believe that all men have this sexual knowledge that is unlimited. They know how to get us turned on, give us an orgasm or two and then cuddle afterwards. When they don't do these things, we get really upset. *How could he not know I want to cuddle afterwards? How could he not know where my clitoris is?* See what I'm getting at? But sometimes they don't know and we do have to tell them.

What's happened with this is that we've been falsely taught by movies and TV and magazines that all men know everything there is to know about sex and then some. If only this were true! But it's not true. It might have come from the whole Playboy/James Bond idea where these types of men can take any woman and give her unlimited sexual pleasure. These men are perfect and they know everything. Most men aren't like these men.

Men, for the most part, are like women. Some of them grew up with parents who taught them that sex was bad, too. Or they became inhibited for whatever reason. Yet, men usually tend to get over this stuff a lot more quickly than women. However, they are still on the same path as we are and that means they have to do as we do: Learn as you go.

I think it's good to know that men don't automatically know "what to do" and that you have to sometimes tell them. It may be a shock to some women to know that men aren't born knowing all about sex and some of them are in the dark as much as we are.

Sure, it's easier to leave it up to your man and let him start doing the "guessing game." But why would you want to make him guess how to please you? Wouldn't it be easier to speak the words out loud and just tell the poor guy what you like? Yes, it's easier to just leave it to him and to chance, but many times, he's just as lost as you are. Also, he doesn't want to do anything that might upset you. What if he touches you in a place that's "forbidden?" Then he gets yelled at and maybe called a few names he'd rather not hear.

Here's where having an open line of communication comes in to help. It might take a few tries, but learn to ask for what you want. Even if it's just guiding his hand somewhere or telling him you want to kiss him, which shows him how to kiss you. Also, learn how to talk about sex with each other. If sex is never discussed, then it will not likely get any better. It's only when we can begin to talk about it that it becomes part of our lives, not just something "naughty" we do with each other in the dark.

Another thing—don't hold back. Ask for what you want. Don't yell or cry, just tell. Usually, the more free you are to *talk* about sex, the easier the sex will come and the easier it will be to orgasm.

Also, don't be afraid to ask for what you want *out* of the bedroom. Say, for instance, that your man wants sex all the time and you wouldn't mind it either. However, there are always massive amounts of laundry to do and you're tired. He wants sex; you want help with the laundry. I see a compromise, don't you?

The truth is that the more you give, the more you get. The same goes for him. Not having your needs met doesn't just mean in the bedroom. And if you're not getting help with the laundry, why would you want to have sex with this guy? Ask for what you need. And then see where it leads. The possibilities are endless.

One last thing, if you're not in the mood for sex, you're not in the mood. No amount of chocolate or foot rubbing is going to get you there, either. So, don't have it unless you totally want it. If you are not in the mood and you try to "force" it, it leads to nothing but trouble. Sometimes, we are just too tired for sex. Sometimes, we just want to sleep instead of having sex. And that's okay. We all live stressful, busy lives. Making sex a priority doesn't mean making it a mandate.

Keep in mind that most men won't want to have sex with you if you're not into it. If you just lie there like a dead fish, he's not going to be exactly thrilled. I know we're all taught that men don't care as long as they "get it." That's a falsehood. Men do care about things like this and if they don't, they don't deserve to have any woman as a lover. Sex is something that is shared between a couple, not something that is forced or expected. If you're only having sex because it's your "wifely duty" then you need to have a talk. And sometimes, that's all it takes to make things better.

However, it is up to you to speak up. If you don't ever tell him how you feel, he won't ever guess, just like he can't guess what turns you on or how to make you orgasm. The ball is in your court. It's how you play it that counts.

CONTROL

In any relationship, there is a power struggle. However, when it comes to sex, it's important to know that most women are in control. We usually say when and where. We have to ability to call it off, if we like, or to not even get started. But after the fun starts, it's usually the man who takes over and is in control.

Most women are fine with handing the reins over to their man once things get going. And that's okay. During sex, there can only be one chief. One person has to be in charge and, usually, it's just sexier for the women to be the submissive. I know I like it. I like having things done to me and not knowing what's going to happen next. I like my man to do a little extra from time to time and surprise me. I also like to fantasize about a man I don't know taking control of me. That doesn't mean I'd allow it to happen in real life, but what does a little fantasy hurt?

So, to me, the issue of control in the bedroom is a non-issue. But knowing that the man is going to take over once the sex begins can help to ease tension and anxiety about sex. Also, if he knows you like it when he takes over, he's going to get very excited and eager to please once things start to heat up. It's also very satisfying to look across the room at your man and know that once the bedroom door closes, he's in control.

Of course, when the sex is over, he converts back to his old self and that means, he's still probably going to be taking the trash out. But that's a given.

However, it doesn't always have to be like this. Sometimes, you can switch it up and tell him what to do and when to do it or you can just push him back and do whatever you like. A woman in control like this is a total sexual turn-on for most men. If you'd rather let him be the boss, that's okay too. You have to find what works for you best and then the control issue becomes a non-issue. And that's a great thing.

FANTASY

Fantasies are gateways into our hidden desires. Fantasies allow us to roam in any arena and do as we like. They let us know a lot about ourselves if we just open ourselves up to them. Fantasy is a great way to explore and give us the nerve to ask for what we want.

All women have their favorite fantasies. I know I do. One involves me, a rock star and a box of donuts. Hey, it's just a fantasy and that means it can be as silly and outrageous as I want.

So, what's your fantasy?

One way to really crank up your libido is to fantasize. Take a fantasy break from time to time and include your favorite guy. Or, include someone you have a crush on, like a rock star or the guy at the coffee place. It doesn't matter who, it just matters that you do it.

By fantasizing, you're opening yourself up more sexually and you begin to recognize that you are a sexual being and you deserve to be sexually satisfied. A fantasy, like I said, can be anything you want. It can go anywhere you want it to go and you don't have to worry about getting pregnant or catching a disease. Many women have BDSM fantasies but would never find themselves in that type of relationship. Many women have fantasies about being submissive but are strong women in their lives. Other women have fantasies that range from being a naughty schoolgirl to a hard-nosed boss. It's just fantasy and it only means that you have an active imagination. It's also a big boost to your libido. Once you become aware that fantasy is an ordinary part of your sex life, you can really start to open up.

And what if you want to try a fantasy out? Hey, try it out. It usually doesn't take much convincing for a man to play along with anything. They are usually more than willing to try anything once. Say, for instance, that you have a fantasy about being tied up or just blindfolded. Try to incorporate it into your sex life. Just give it a try, but only give it a try with someone you truly trust. There's nothing more embarrassing than being tied up and left. You don't want that. It could be a little embarrassing.

Also, a good way to engage your fantasies is to read erotica. There are lots of books out there that deal with all kinds of sexual fantasies and just reading about them is a way to open that window up a little. Sure, they're fictitious characters, but the idea behind the erotica is sexual freedom, something that most of us crave deep, down inside. All bookstores carry these types of books are there are, literally, thousands to choose from. So, if you are hesitant to try something out in your real life, let a character in a book try it out for you. Another good thing about erotica is that it is a total libido enhancer. Nothing can get you going quite like reading erotica. It's as good an aphrodisiac as any.

The point is to engage your fantasy life and then allow it lead you where it may. Your real desires are buried deep inside of you and this is one way to bring them out, by using your imagination. By doing this, you're allowing your mind to open up to all the possibilities that are out there for you to enjoy. And, of course, that leads to less inhibition and really, really good sex. So, never discount the powerful effects of fantasy and where it can take you. You might just surprise yourself and turn your fantasy into a reality. And that can be very satisfying.

Why not give it a try?

THE WAY YOU LOOK TONIGHT

One of the most inhibiting factors to a good sex life is the way we women feel about our bodies. All of us have flaws and things we don't like about ourselves. We all worry about the "fat" on our bellies and our "monstrous" thighs. One of the problems with this, other than the fact that it's very silly and counterproductive, is that we usually tend to amplify our faults. In addition to that, some of even imagine that we have more flaws than we do. Why do we do this? It's anyone's guess. Maybe we're looking for reassurance or maybe we just like to bash ourselves.

However, when we focus too much on "what's wrong" with our bodies, we stop focusing on "what's right" about our relationships. And when this happens, we start wanting to keep everything covered up and the lights turned out. And that leads to a non-existent sex life.

You might feel uncomfortable with sex because you might be "ashamed" of the way you look. Want to know something? He doesn't really care what you "look" like. I mean, he cares, but he's not going to judge you. In case you've forgotten, he's probably seen you naked before. And, another thing, as long as you are naked, he's happy. All men seem to operate on the same principles and one of these principles is: If she's naked, I might get lucky. He's only thinking about having sex. Believe me, he's not thinking about the size of your thighs. And, if he is, he might just be gay. So what if you gained a few pounds? Big deal. It's not him that's putting that pressure on you to look perfect, it's you.

I've heard that women don't wear make-up for men; they wear it for other women. Same thing with clothes. We're only dressing up to make other women jealous of us. (If nothing else, this bit of information might save you some money on shoes.) Sounds weird but think about it. Most men do not like heavy make-up. I've heard a few even say they like the natural look—no make-up at all. This means, he likes you just the way you are, with all your "faults," real *or* imagined. He loves you and that means every single part of you.

Don't wear clothing for other women; wear it for your man. Go out and buy something that makes you feel sexy, even if it's just a little tank and panties. Even if it's a long nightgown. Buy one in silk and don't wear anything under it. This will feel like heaven and then think about his hands on you, moving along the bodice and then down... You can take it from there.

Keep in mind that it's hard to get busy if you're worried about the rolls of fat on your tummy. Everyone has rolls of fat on their tummies! Who cares if you have a few pounds to lose or would like a boob job? Do what you can to improve your body and then let it be what it is: A vessel to move you from here to there and a pleasure palace.

So I say stop worrying about the way you look. Instead, concentrate on what's right about your body, not what's "wrong." As I said, he doesn't really care what you look like, he's just happy that you're there with him.

THE ELUSIVE ORGASM

Before we go any further, let's talk about the orgasm. For some women, it is quite elusive. I've heard that many women never have an orgasm when they have sex. They are orgasm-less. And the odd thing about it is, they seem perfectly content to be this way! Now, in my opinion, that's a crime. No woman on this earth should go without orgasms.

Here's how to tell if you've had an orgasm: If you "don't know" if you've had one, you probably haven't had one. Because if you've had one, you definitely know it. It's not something that you forget easily.

If you're having a hard time having an orgasm, know that you're not alone. I was astonished to find out one of my very best friends has only had a few orgasms in her life. And she's got four kids!

It's worth mentioning that you might want to see your doctor and make sure everything is okay before you start worrying about not having orgasms. However, if everything checks out at the doctor and you're still having a hard time reaching orgasm, then you might just have a mental block. Usually, the orgasm is there, waiting to come out. You might just have to coax it a bit.

In a way, I think many women who claim to not have had orgasms have actually had them but haven't recognized them as such. I think they have probably had them—in their sleep. Call it the female equivalent of the wet dream. Have you ever woken up with your hands between your legs?

Have you ever had a sex dream and woken up feeling very sexy? More than likely, your body is taking over and you're having nocturnal orgasms. I know that I was having orgasms before I even started having sex and didn't even know it. One day, I had an "Ah ha!" moment when I realized I had been having them all along, in my sleep.

But if you're not sure if you've had one, sit down and think about it. Some women don't even know what they "feel" like. (I didn't.) There are many ways to describe them and, of course, orgasms feel different to each person. I've heard that some feel like a tickling sensation. To me, it's a feeling of letting go of everything to just enjoy a sensation of total ecstasy.

Here's another way I describe them: Just when you are about to give up on getting one and just give your body over to the sensations you're feeling, it starts at you. There's a little tingle that brings everything into focus. After the tingle starts, there's the anticipation of it, how soon it will come and how long it'll last. Then it just grips and overtakes you and there's not a thing you can do but hold on for the ride. And once it's gone, you're sad to see it go.

Is that how you feel? If not, maybe you should re-think your stand on orgasms. They don't always have to be the same. I know mine are very intense with a vibrator but having one during sex is the absolute best.

Orgasms should be as much as a goal for women as they are men. I've heard that female orgasms are, in fact, helpful in getting the egg fertilized. So, there is a function for it. It's not just for fun, though that is a great aspect to it.

Another thing to realize is that you are in control of your orgasm, not your lover. Shock! Disbelief? It's true. He can help, but he can't have it for you. Nor can he "give" it to you. It's yours for the taking. And you have to take it.

Remember that it's not all about pleasing him—it's also about pleasing *yourself* first. If you do that, you will automatically please him.

There is a big secret to being good in bed. Wanna know what it is? Relax! Just relax and enjoy it. Stop worrying about the bills and the pills and that alarm clock. Don't go searching for that orgasm, it will find you when you're ready.

The biggest thing to keep in mind is to be receptive to what he's giving you. If you can receive what he wants to give, you've got it. One way to do this is to feel sexy. Once you feel sexy, you'll want him like nothing else. It's easy to feel sexy. You can wear lingerie that makes you feel sexy or you can read some erotica or you can delve off into fantasy land for a few minutes before you have sex. Imagine yourself as a sex goddess and soon you will *be* a sex goddess. And being receptive and feeling sexy will open you up to intense orgasms.

You might even be surprised to know that most women are multi-orgasmic. I can do this with my vibrator. I get one off and then I just have to have two or sometimes three more. During sex, I just enjoy the aftershocks of the orgasm as my man finishes doing his thing.

The good thing about sex—and orgasms—is that the more you do it, the more you *want* to do it. It's like chocolate but without the calories. Sexual intensity is a choice, not a condition. It's up to you.

FIRST THINGS FIRST

Your vagina. Yeah, we're going *there.* Well, you are, at least.

If you think about it, the vagina has been called every name in the book. There are so many euphemisms for it, it's hard to keep up with all of them. Take a minute and think about all the things you've heard it called.

That many, huh?

What do you call yours? For some reason, I have a funny feeling you don't refer to it at all. Things are about to change.

Again, think of some of the euphemisms for the vagina; let them roll around your head for a moment or two. If any of these "terms" make you feel uncomfortable and uneasy, just write them down and stare at them. Eventually they will become just words to you. I believe when we take offense to derogatory terms, we are inevitably setting ourselves up to dislike not only sex itself, but our own sex organs. And these terms describe exactly that, our sex organs. Yes, they can be a little crass, but there's nothing any of us can do to change this. These terms have been around a lot longer than any of us have. However, we can change our attitude towards these words and that, in effect, turns these words into just that—words. And that can help a girl let down her guard and start feeling her sexuality. And that can lead to an amazing sex life.

If you can begin to own your sexuality, and that includes your vagina, you are going to experience so much freedom that you'll wonder why you objected to these silly terms in the first place.

We don't even talk about our vaginas and going to the gynecologist is one of our most dreaded yearly activities. Why? We should be proud of that thing. Women have so much power in their vaginas it's unbelievable. That's where life comes from! Just think about it. If it weren't for vaginas there wouldn't be a single person walking around on this earth.

But for some reason, none of us make friends with ours. Even the word, vagina, sounds weird coming out of your mouth. It's like Va-gi-na. Ick. Penis even sounds better than that, doesn't it? And that's probably because a man named it. A woman would have given it a much better name. Like Lily or some other flower.

Today, make friends with your vagina. Men do it with their penises all the time, don't they? They even refer to it as their buddy and give it names. Why don't women do this? Well, it's kinda weird and a little awkward. And, besides, who has the time? Make time for your girl. Make time to get to know her.

Get a mirror, lie down and meet your new best friend. I mean it. Go get a mirror, find some private space and take a look. Huh? Wow. I mean...*wow*. The first time I saw mine was back in college and I was nineteen or so. My boyfriend was more acquainted with my vagina than I was. I didn't even know if I liked the way it looked. There was so much stuff going on down there I didn't know where it began or where it ended. However, I must say I was impressed with it, even if it did somewhat intimidate me. Over time, though, I came to be more comfortable with it and that meant I was more comfortable with my whole self. Yet, had I never had that initial peek at it, I might have continued to pretend it didn't exist or come to realize that it could give me so much pleasure.

Vaginas, like breasts, come in all shapes and sizes. Some vaginas have a little extra skin and some don't. Just like our faces, some have thin lips and some thick. They're all different and each has unique characteristics.

Not liking your body, including your "delicate flower," is a one way ticket to disowning it and when you do this, it only spells trouble. It also means sexual inhibition. So, learn to love what's yours. Own it as you own the rest of your body and love everything about it. There is nothing "wrong" with it and it doesn't look or smell "funny." *It's your vagina.* Owning leads not only to sexual power but to sexual freedom and that leads to overcoming sexual shyness.

Now, after you've met your vagina, meet the rest of your body. Go to the mirror and strip naked. Look at yourself. That's you standing there wondering what you're doing. That's you and you are the best thing in the world. You should always think of yourself like that. Confidence is everything. Without it, all this crazy stuff starts happening, like a lack of good sex. You don't want that, now, do you?

YOU TOUCH YOURSELF: MASTURBATION 101

Someone once said that it's very important to know thyself. One of the best ways to get to know yourself is to know how you like to be touched. And where. And for how long. And with what intensity. One good way to do that is to touch yourself.

This can be tough, especially if you've never done it.

So, now that you're getting along well with your new friends, your vagina and your body, you're going to take it a step farther. You're going to please your new friends and, in turn, they're going to please you. A whole bunch.

A big hindrance to a good sex life is that we tend to get locked into patterns of sexual behavior, doing it the same way all the time. It doesn't have to be like this at all. We get into long-term relationships and the sex spark begins to fade. Believe me, it doesn't have to. One way to lose some of your inhibition is to start masturbating on a regular basis. Once you know what sensations feel good to you, then you can show him. And, better yet, you will know how to find that place again. *Yes, you can do this*. Even if you have to have all the lights out, show him what feels good to you. One way to turn any man into jelly is to touch yourself in front of him. You might have to work up to this, though.

First of all, you might want to realize that your man masturbates. Probably more than a few times a week. No, it isn't because he doesn't like you anymore. It's because he's a man and men are gonna do it no matter what. Besides, you *want* him to masturbate. The more he does it, the more practice he has at doing a good job once you're having fun under the sheets.

So if he gets to do it all the time, why don't you?

If you're one of the few women who have not yet partaken of the delights of masturbation, then my suggestion to you is to buy a vibrator. You can get one over the internet—there are literally hundreds of websites that sell all kinds of vibrators. Small, large, anything you want. Buy one that offers penetration *and* clitoral stimulation. They go by the name of "Beaver Twister" or "Rabbit" and come in "discreet" packages. Some also go by the name "muscle massager" and they not only help tired muscles, but can give intense orgasms. These types are available at just about any store and really do the trick. All you have to do is put it between you legs, turn it on and *bam!* Instant pleasure! Pick the one you feel most comfortable with and get prepared to get busy.

Now let's talk about doing it. Unfortunately, I know many women who don't masturbate and a few have even said things like, "I have a husband, I don't have to do *that*," as if it disgusts them.

Apparently, they haven't done it or they wouldn't have that attitude.

When was the last time you did it? And if you say, I never have... Well, you don't know what you're missing.

One way to lose inhibition and overcome shyness is to pleasure yourself. I will be honest and say that before I married, I didn't masturbate. I wasn't "raised" like that. My thinking was that the man was there for a reason and he could give me an orgasm, but I couldn't give it to myself. Touching myself, bringing myself to orgasm...well, *that* was a little *too much*.

However, I came to realize it was not *too much* and that I needed to masturbate if I was ever going to get in touch with myself. (No pun intended.) If you want to be more sexually empowered, you are going to have to start pleasuring yourself. It doesn't take much. Once you've got your vibrator—any kind will do—take an hour off from everything and go to it. You don't have to tell anyone what you're doing, just say you've got a headache and are going to lie down for a while and that you don't want to be disturbed. (Be sure to lock the door!)

And go lie down—with your vibrator. If you've never experienced an orgasm with a vibrator before, you'll be coming back for more. And as you're masturbating, have a fantasy or two. If you like some guy off a TV show, fantasize about him. Or you can fantasize about your lover, your husband, your boyfriend. It doesn't matter who you fantasize about and you don't even have to fantasize if you don't want to. Just take the time to pleasure yourself. This will benefit you more than you can imagine.

If you don't "feel" like it or feel guilt, then let it go. Just lie there and maybe have a fantasy or two without doing anything. Don't force it to come, just think about something pleasurable, like getting a backrub. Then allow your mind to lead to what it naturally will. Now place the vibrator where it will give you the most pleasure, turn it on and see what happens. Keep in mind that with a vibrator, you don't have to force the orgasm. Many times, they will just jump out of you, sending waves of pleasure up and down your body.

Of course, getting to this state of ecstasy might take a few tries. So, take a little time and work at it until you find out what makes you orgasm. Don't be afraid to experiment, either. You might buy a "Beaver Twister" and a "muscle massager" and find that you like the "muscle massager" best. Or you might want to try a newer model. That's okay. Just do whatever feels good to you. That's what this is all about—making yourself feel good through masturbation.

After you've practiced for a while and if you have the guts and really want to drive your man wild, let him watch as you masturbate. It will make you feel vulnerable and tingly all over. And that might lead to other exciting things.

Men love to watch. They are visual creatures, after all. Men love women; they really do, so get over the idea that he wouldn't want you to do "anything" like that. In fact, he probably not only wants it, he wants to be in there with you while you're doing it.

So, why not let him watch you go at it? You can keep all the lights off, if you wish. Just knowing you're doing it is probably enough to send him into a frenzy. Now once you've got your groove on, and feel comfortable enough, it's time to let your man take a turn at the control. Men love to play with sex toys. They love to give you intense pleasure. It makes them feel like they're "the man." Get in touch with your body first and then show him how to do it.

If you have a guy that doesn't respond well to this, know that he is insecure. You might have to coax him into it using your open line of communication I spoke of in an earlier chapter. Once he's done it, it's all he'll want to do for a while. You've been warned.

A FOX IN SHEEP'S CLOTHING

Women are different from men and one way we show it is by how we dress. We can do that in sexy clothes. Once we dress sexy, we can begin to feel sexy, which is just a precursor to *being* sexy. Once we feel sexy, we *are* sexy.

It's no secret that we all want men to look and lust after us. That's why we dress up and put on cellulite cream and spends hundreds—if not thousands—of dollars a year to appear attractive. And we do it even if we're married with kids. Once we stop doing it, we let part of ourselves die. We forget our sexuality. That's sad. One should never, ever think of herself as unattractive or undesirable.

So, I suggest you go out and buy a few sexy clothes, even if you just wear them around your lover. Put them on and model in front of him. Let him tell you how sexy you look. And don't wait to do this if you're trying to lose weight. Seeing yourself in a sexy way means accepting yourself. And it might just give you more incentive to lose those extra pounds.

Dress in a way that is so enticing it will make your man want to rip the clothes off your back—with your permission, of course. Accentuate the positive. If you have great breasts, show 'em off. If you have a nice butt, go for it. Legs? Short skirts always do the trick. And you should know by now that most men love high heels on a woman.

Never apologize for your sexuality or for wearing clothes that you like, even if they don't fit well or people stare at you. If you like them, wear them. I think there is way too much of an emphasis put on clothing and the way we dress—or don't dress. Do what feels good to you. Like I said, even if you just wear the clothes around the house, do it. Feel like a woman again. Give yourself permission to be sexy.

Now, go buy some really sexy lingerie. Meet him at the door in it. (If you have kids, send them to a babysitter when you do this.) Wow. Get ready for some mind-blowing sex. Buy some of those stripper shoes and open the door with a smile.

Or, even better, open the door naked.

PORN—YES, HE HAS A PRIVATE STASH

For some reason, many women have a hard time grappling with the idea that their man looks at and/or watches porn. I feel this warrants mentioning because if you can come to an understanding of it, then you can avoid many fights and live a happier life. You can also lose a lot of your insecurity.

The fact of the matter is that most men love porn. Yes, they do, even if they tell you they don't like it, they do. They're only telling you this so you won't get upset and start a fight. This doesn't mean you have to bring it up or whatever, but it does mean if you find his secret stash, learn to deal with it and shrug it off. And, if you're with a man for any length of time, you're going to find his secret stash. It's inevitable.

Some women feel hurt over the whole porn thing but that's just silly. He's not looking at it and comparing you to those women. Believe me, he's not. He's looking at it because men love to look at naked women. Given the choice, most men would love to see every single woman in the world—young and old—naked at some point.

But why? Who knows why? It's in their genetic makeup if you ask me. It's just something that's ingrained in them to do. Accept that and your man will think you are the coolest chick in the world. This doesn't mean you have to share it with him and if it makes you uncomfortable, just don't bring it up. But know that his looking at porn doesn't have a thing to do with you and it doesn't mean he doesn't like or desire you anymore. It simply means he likes porn. That's pretty much it, too.

SPANKING THE MONKEY

As I mentioned briefly earlier, your man more than likely masturbates. Of course, he probably calls it "spanking the monkey" or something juvenile like that. So, yeah, he masturbates even when you're having sex all the time. Why? Because he's a man, that's why. For some reason, some women get really crazy over this. There's no need. Look at it this way: If he masturbates on a regular basis, he'll be able to last longer when you have sex. Look at it like he's practicing.

All you have to do to not let little stuff like this bother you is to accept that if you're with a man—a real man— these two things are things he does *for him* and usually he does them on the sly. It doesn't have a thing to do with you or with his desire for you. In fact, it probably makes him want you even more. Again, with feeling, *his masturbating has nothing to do with you.* It's all about him. So, don't get mad at him over this. Let him have it and be that cool chick who doesn't let silly little things like this bring her down. It's completely unnecessary misery.

Look at it this way—his masturbating is firing up his engine. Therefore, it's just a precursor to what you two do between the sheets. Be glad that he does it, that way he's more than ready to handle what you throw at him. Therefore, his masturbating isn't just beneficial to him, it can be beneficial to you as well.

So, forget what he does and how many times he does it. Instead of worrying about what he's doing, do it yourself.

Yes, you too, can masturbate, if not daily, then weekly. If you're both getting off by masturbation, the sex, more than likely, will intensify. That's because once you work through these silly issues, you stop caring about this insignificant stuff and start working on the best stuff, like having a really good sex life, which is beneficial to both of you.

THE PROBLEM WITH PORN (THERE DOESN'T HAVE TO BE ONE)

Now that you're aware of your man's private porno stash, why not check it out and see what all the fuss is about? Oh, don't freeze up now. Just sit back and listen.

Porn isn't just out there for the viewing pleasure of perverts and degenerates. It can actually be a viable tool in a good sex life for most couples. It can turn a girl on just as easily as it can turn a guy on. However, most guys don't have the hang-ups most girls do and, I guess, that's why guys usually love it and women usually hate it. Hence, the problem with porn.

Pornography is a very sensitive subject for most women. If they find out that their man is watching it, there's usually hell to pay and a lot of tears to shed. It's such a volatile subject with some women, it can't even be brought up, lest they have a freak-out. Women can get incredibly resentful over porn. I should know. I used to feel the same way.

And it was mostly due to my own insecurities. I thought that the only reason my husband would want to watch porn was because he thought I was ugly and fat. The fact of the matter was, I was neither of the two but that didn't stop me from banning him from watching porn.

I used to hate it. I used to think it objectified women and there was something wrong with people getting paid to have sex on film. But then something happened. I got curious about it myself. I don't know why, but one day I began to think about porn. It wasn't an obsession or anything; I just began to question my objections to it. Before this, anytime my husband wanted to share in the erotic delights of porn, I would cringe and say, "No!"

I think it was because I thought if I watched porn, I would turn into a slut or whore or something like that. Just seeing it might make me a bad girl. But, as I soon realized, maybe porn wasn't such a bad thing.

As I said, most men love porn and my husband was no exception. He wasn't obsessed with it or anything, but he did like to view it from time to time. Though we rarely watched porn together, I had "allowed" him to purchase a few. I was trying to be a "cool" girl, even though I did secretly resent it. One day, when he was out of the house, I thought about his stash. Without thinking, I went upstairs and found it, then went through the tapes, pulling a random one out. Then, I popped it in and started to watch.

I must say, it took my breath away at first. Is that what we really look like when we're making love?! It was almost embarrassing. All those arms and legs and penises and breasts going everywhere and all at once made my head spin. It looked so *real*. It wasn't shot for artistic reasons; it was shot to show sex at its most basic nature. And that nature was hard to look away from.

To say the least, it really opened my mind. I didn't tell my husband that I had watched one of his tapes, but I began to do it more often, just to test myself, just to see if it would eventually win me over. After a while, it did. And then I was able to watch one with my husband. I must say the porn wasn't on for five minutes before we were going at it.

I think one of the main reasons women don't like porn is simply because they think their man is comparing them to the girl in the video. For some men, this might be the case, but for a lot, it's just a chance to see another chick getting it on. As I've said, men are very visual creatures. And men separate their love lives from porn scenes more than we give them credit for. They're not usually watching it because they don't like their lovers anymore. They're watching it because men, in general, love sex and that means they love to watch others getting it on. I think they take it less seriously than we do. It's something they enjoy and like to watch, so what's the big deal?

That may be a bit too much to take, but it's true. And, why judge them over it? It's in their nature. Why should they be asked to change it? Sure, some people can take it overboard and then it takes over their lives. But, I think the harder you pull at something, the less likely it is to give. If you keep hammering at him to give it up, that makes him want to hold on even more. If you relax a bit and try to share it with him, then maybe it becomes less of a big deal. It becomes something you can share as a couple, not something he has to sneak off and do in secret.

I've gotten so relaxed about porn now that my husband rarely even looks at it anymore. (At least that's what he tells me.) See what I'm saying though? Once you stop making a big deal of it, he'll probably stop making a big deal, too.

Sure, women are less visual creatures than men and that may be one reason we tend to see porn as being too graphic. For some of us, it is a bit much. However, when you boil it down, it's just sex, that's all it is. It's sex that was filmed and then packaged and sold to a viewing audience. There will always be a market for it, like it or not. You don't have to condone it nor do you have to condemn it. The big thing is that you shouldn't be resentful of it.

Another reason women have trouble with porn is because the way they perceive the women in the porns as being seen as objects. They see it as degrading not just to the woman in the porn, but to all women in general. This isn't so. Just because some chick has sex on film for money doesn't mean I'm going to and that doesn't mean you're going to, either. Also, the women in these films are not coerced into doing it. They have to sign contracts; therefore, they know what they are getting into. Do these critics know that the women in porn usually get paid a lot more than the men? It's one of the few professions where this actually happens!

Perhaps it's not your ideas that make you feel this way, but it's the ideal that comes from society that porn, and sometimes sex, is bad. Usually, we only know something is bad when we are told it's bad. You don't have to be like these people. As I've said, you own your body and your mind and soul. If you don't like porn, hey, you don't like it. However, if you can grow to like it, it can be used as a tool to spice things up.

Porn is one of my all-time favorite aphrodisiacs. Pop a DVD in and I'm ready to go in about five minutes. Even if my libido is at an all-time low and especially if my favorite porn actor is getting busy.

If you're uneasy with porn and just don't like the idea of it, you can do what I mentioned above. Get a DVD and then watch it. It won't change you, believe me. It's not going to make that big of an impression on you. But if you relax and just give it a chance, you might actually like it. And if you don't, at least you gave it a chance.

So, why not give it a try? If you don't like certain scenes, you can just fast-forward until you find one you like. I, personally, like the one-on-one scenes the best. Lots of kissing is good, too. Yet most porn is made for men and we all know men and women see things in a different light so that means there is usually more penetration than kissing.

But that doesn't mean you have to discount it. You can learn to like, if not love, porn as much as the next guy.

Tip: You buy the porn and ask him if he wants to watch a movie. Pop it and watch his eyes bug out. Hey, you might even want to be *his* porn star for a night. I mean, why not?

But even after you've given it a chance and you're still not into it? Why not watch a sexy movie or two? Yes, there are some out there, but sexy movies are becoming a rarity in Hollywood. Used to be, you could get to see some sex in a movie. Rarely, these days, do you ever see any mainstream movie where the characters are doing anything resembling sex.

However, there are a few older movies out there and if you want to invest the time with plot to get to the "good" parts, here are a few more artistic films that turn up the heat:

- *Henry and June*
- *Last Tango in Paris*
- *The Lover*
- *Bound*

All I'm saying is, don't knock it till you try it. Porn can be an aphrodisiac and it's a whole lot more effective than oysters.

KISSING IS A GOOD THING

Kissing is a good thing. And, as we all know, all good things start with kissing. And, also, kissing is always better than not kissing.

Knowing yourself and knowing how you like to be kissed is essential to good sex. Kissing is the gateway to erotic delights. It gets everything going and intensifies the sex as it heats up. Everyone loves kissing and everyone loves to do it.

Different cultures have different practices of kissing. We all know that the Eskimos rub noses—perhaps so their tongues don't get frozen together?—and, of course, we all know what the French started.

Kissing is one of those things that is so utterly necessary for good sex but somehow, sometimes gets put on the backburner. A kiss can lead to so many good things it's unbelievable. It can lead to electric sex and it can bond two people together.

But a bad kisser is just plain bad news.

If you don't like the way your man kisses, kiss him in the way you want to be kissed. Just say, "Let me kiss you," and then do it. Now, tell him to kiss you like that. I, personally, love it when my man grabs the back of my head and pulls me to him, like he isn't about to let me go. I love that! It's so manly and sexually charged.

Once you're lip-locked, you can run your tongue along his teeth. You can lick, kiss, nibble at the lips to get him—and you—revved up. When you're done with the lips, go down to the neck. Men love to be touched as much as we love it. They certainly won't come out and say that, but they do.

A good thing to keep in mind is that a relaxed but firm tongue is necessary for a good kiss. No hard pointy tongues! That doesn't do anything for anyone. One way to visualize this is to realize that an open mouth kiss should have *relaxed* lips. Once you can relax the lips, you can relax everything and get what you're after and what you're after is a "weak in the knees" moment," which are always sure to follow a really great kiss.

I LOVE YOU

I think it is so important to tell the one you're gonna love on that you love him. Unless, of course, you don't. Then you don't have to say anything at all.

By interjecting this little sentence into your lovemaking, you are going to turn the heat up. If you want to really get your man going, tell him you love him while you're making love. Just look into his eyes and say, "I love you." That will do it. And that will help intensify the sex tenfold. And, he might just say it back.

But some people are hesitant to do this. Why? Because people are afraid of this word. Movies have taught us that it is the ultimate commitment. Once you say it to someone, there's no getting out. However, I think it just means you care a lot. And you either care about someone or you don't.

Love is a very simple human emotion. It really is. It's just that we've been programmed to think that it's extremely complicated but it isn't. The emotion behind love is where the power lies.

So, I say if you love your man, tell him you love him. And you know whether you do or not. Sure, you do run the risk of him not saying it back, but that doesn't mean he doesn't feel it. Some men are just weird about this word and feel that if they say it, it means something other than the emotion behind it. However, if you say it to him and he doesn't like to say it, just keep on and he'll eventually start. Just give him time to absorb this new word and let him respond when he feels the need. There's no need to rush him. But, then again, there's no need to deny how you feel either.

LET HIM WORSHIP YOUR BODY: FOREPLAY 101

If you know your own body and what turns you on, you can have good sex anytime, anywhere. A precursor to good sex is good foreplay. Your body had erogenous zones that often get overlooked. If you can identify your own personal erogenous zones, you can help your lover do the same and that will lead to really hot sex.

Good foreplay is like chocolate—most women can't get enough. One reason might be because many women reach orgasm during foreplay and the rest of the sex is just icing on the cake. However, getting to good foreplay might be difficult for some as it means that your body will be seen— and felt—at all angles. For many women, this can lead to shyness because of body image issues. As I've mentioned, most of us have a few insecurities about our bodies. Not many of us look like supermodels and we all have flaws. We want to know that our men like, if not love, every single part of us. We want them to look at us as if we're the *only* woman on earth. We really, really do. Even if it's just for an hour or so at a time, we want to be the center of our man's world. This means we want our men to worship our bodies. And by worship I mean, we want them to love every single part of us, even our flaws. If they touch and kiss and love our flaws, that usually means they love us. And that usually leads to good sex. One good way to do this is to have him touch you everywhere, concentrating on areas that sometimes get overlooked.

All you have to do in order to get some good foreplay is to show up and become the center of his world for a space of time. Take the time and *allow* him to worship your body. All you have to do is sit back and let the worship begin. It doesn't hurt if he compliments you from time to time, either. But you can't come out and ask for something like this, can you?

I say, why not? What we women tend to forget is that we're in a relationship with straight men and straight men rarely have any clue about anything having to do with a woman. Men rarely understand why stuff like this is so important to us. But all they have to know is that it *is* important. If you've got a good man, he should be more than willing to do a little body worship from time to time.

Body worship is a great way for him to not only get your juices flowing, but for him to become aware of what you like and what you don't. If you can ask him to touch you a certain way, he'll eventually learn that's what you want. Having open communication about your sex life can be intimidating at first, but after a while, it becomes second nature. Of course, never bark at him to do something and, if he's not doing it right, show him how you want to be touched. Also, please don't huff or eye roll when you're doing this. This will lead to him getting turned-off. He wants to please you, but he doesn't want to be treated like a child. So, go gently with him and let him know what really turns you on.

This makes for excellent foreplay.

But, first of all, he should begin by concentrating on your whole body. Most men just dive in for the breasts or the vagina. If you let him know you have other body parts, he can explore those as well.

Here is a guide that describes various body parts that usually get overlooked. If you explore them first and see what kind of touch you like, later on you can guide his hand to these areas and show him how to touch you. Like I said, this makes for excellent foreplay and really gets all of your senses going. And that leads to really good sex.

A guide to erotic zones on the body:

- *Your stomach:* This zone needs to be stroked lightly and kissed gently—no sucking action needed.
- *Your chest:* This is not referring to your breasts. This is the zone above your breasts that doesn't usually get much attention and is highly erotic. Just having a hand running across it can give a girl goosebumps.
- *Your breasts:* Breasts are a highly erotic zone, maybe even *the* most erotic zone, and some women can even have orgasms by having their breasts rubbed and kissed. Have him run his hands under your breasts, like he's scooping them up, then have him press his face into them.
- *Your legs:* Have him run his hands up and down your legs, then between the thighs. However, don't allow him to go near your vagina just yet. This is titillation and this action will soon make you want more.
- *Your Feet:* All feet need a good rub from time to time, but while you're engaging in foreplay, just a gently stroke along the arch. If he likes, he can give them a few kisses.
- *Your back:* If he likes, he can kiss his way up and down your back, sucking gently as he does so.
- *Your buttocks:* Having your buttocks stroked during sex can intensify an orgasm. He can even slide his hands between them from time to time.

- *Your ears:* A light tongue lick along the outer ear is a big turn-on, but no ramming the tongue in.
- *Your neck:* If you have a good neck kisser, good sex is always inevitable. You can practice kissing his neck first, then have him do the same to you. A good sucking motion with an open mouth is best.
- *Your face:* Nice, gently stokes along your cheekbones is always nice.
- *Your underarms:* Yes, your armpits are a highly erotic zone. Having a tongue slide down your armpit during sex is hot. Of course, some might not like this one, but don't knock it until you try it.

Just focusing on these areas can really heat a session up. You can practice on him and then have him do the same to you. Have fun with it.

DOIN' IT DOGGIE STYLE

Doggie style. He wants it but you ain't having it.

One way to get what you want in bed is to give a little of what he wants. And, yes, he wants it doggie style. He wouldn't be a man if he didn't. And if you do for him, he might have to do something special for you sometime, too. So, why not try it a few times and lose a bit of that inhibition about this position? Once you learn how to do it right, you might just start asking him to do it.

I know there's something about doing it doggie that many women just don't like. Maybe we think it's vulgar or low class or trashy. However, this might be one of the reasons this position is so hot. It is kinda crass and it is kinda trashy. But you know what else it is? It's hot and, if and when you can get into it, it really feels good.

However, if he wants you up on all fours, it doesn't help if he asks—or begs—does it? No. In fact, if this is a position you don't like, no amount of cajoling will do the trick. It might be one of those positions you detest for whatever reason. However, if you've never done it, don't knock it until you try it. Why not let him do it like this just once and see if you like it? It can be a really mind-blowing position.

All you have to do to get ready for this position is to turn away from your man and allow him to kiss the back of your neck. Now, climb up onto all fours and allow him to kiss your back and rub your buttocks. Then, he will settle behind you, push your legs open a little and enter you. As he rides you, he can lean forward and rub your breasts and kiss the back of your neck. He can also put his hand between your legs and allow you to rub against it. And let nature take its course.

One good thing to add to this mix is a vibrator. (The "muscle massager" vibrators work best with this.) This gives you both a lot of extra pleasure. As he's riding you, have your vibrator handy and then put it between your legs. This will surely double your pleasure. Be warned, though, he might come rather quickly when you apply the vibrator. (He can feel it, too, and sometimes, it might be too much for him. So don't be surprised...)

This position is good for the woman because it gives you a lot of pressure. And if you add a vibrator into the mix, it's simply delightful.

A MIND-BLOWING POSITION

There are tons of great positions out there, but this has to be one of the best. I like to call it the Modified Doggie. This position is not only good for him, but for you too because each of you gets a little of what you need with this one. And that will certainly make your sex life better.

Start in the doggie position and then lie down until you are flat on your belly, then have your lover spread your legs and enter you from behind. Now he will wriggle his hand until it is flat on your vagina, near your clitoris. Make sure that his hand is still and just move against it. While he rides you, you will ride his hand. Keep the kissing up and if he can get to a breast, have him kiss on it. It won't take long for both of you to come.

THE SQUEEZE

As I motioned in a previous chapter, one reason I believe that women love foreplay is because that's when most reach orgasm. Many women don't reach orgasm through intercourse. I've even heard some women say, "I can't tell you the last time I had an orgasm while having intercourse."

I'll tell you when the last time was for me. It was the last time I did it. Maybe that might change but I hope to God it doesn't. And, the thing is, it's not that hard to do once you get the hang of it.

Getting to good sex isn't that hard when you know how your body works. One way to find out how your body works, and what you like best, is to try new things. So, why not try having an orgasm during sex?

There is nothing better than having an orgasm during intercourse. An orgasm like this totally takes over your body and, afterwards, there's not much you can do but gasp for air and want it all over again.

As I've said, it's not that hard to achieve this. But, be warned—your lover might come quickly when you first start to do this. It might take a few tries to get it right. But if done right, this little move will blow both of your minds.

I simply like to call it *The Squeeze*. Some might call it *The Hold*. You can call it anything you want to but know if you do it, you're going to call it heavenly. Do this to him and you will have a mind-blowing orgasm. And he will never forget it.

As you are having sex—on your back, as it doesn't really work that well on top or doggie—tell him to hold still for a minute while he's deep into you. Now squeeze your vagina around his penis. (Kinda like doing a Kegel, which is a bladder strengthening exercise that mimics holding your urine.) Now you are going to use his penis in the same way you do a vibrator. Clamp onto it and ride him, squeezing your vagina as you move, and grind against him. If you do it right, it won't take long before you have a massive orgasm. You might even have a massive scream rip out of your throat. That's how powerful they can be.

One way to vary this is to put your legs up on his shoulders and have him ride you that way. This gets really deep vaginal penetration. As he's riding you, take your hand and rub your clitoris. Soon, you'll both be coming. Probably verbally.

And, don't just jump up afterwards and run into the bathroom. Hold each other and caress each other's bodies. And, while you're at it, tell each other how much you love one another.

TALK DIRTY TO ME, BABY

Tired of being a good girl? Well, you can still be a good girl during the day but you don't have to be one in the bedroom or with the person you love. You can be a bad, bad girl and one way to be a bad girl is to talk dirty.

It's an art form—talking dirty. It's husky, it's passionate, friendly, and flirty. It signals the tease in all of us and allows us to lose our inhibitions and really get into sex. It allows the bad girl in all of us to come out and play. Everyone should try it at least once.

Good sex doesn't have to be about role playing and fantasy. But it never hurts to mix it up a little. Mixing it up with a little dirty talk will surely rev him up.

So, give it a try. But go easy at first. Know this: You are going to be nervous. More than likely you are going to put your foot in your mouth. But if you do, just ignore it, then he'll ignore it and you can get back on track. Not sure where to start? I've composed a little dialogue that might help…

As you're kissing, whisper in his ear, "I love the way you feel right now."

He will respond in turn.

Now start licking his neck and as you do that, whisper huskily, "Like that?"

"Ummm…" he responds.

"Tell me what I can do to turn you on."

Listen and then do it. More than likely it's not going to be anything you can't handle.

After you do it, get a little more graphic and say something like, "Take me into the bedroom and fuck me."

If that doesn't make his jaw drop, I don't know what would. Maybe this would be better, "Take me into the bedroom and fuck my brains out."

Whoa, mamacita! You're getting the hang of it now.

And as you're doing it, ask him to tell you how it feels. Ask him to verbalize it, then you can verbalize how you feel, with the naughtiest words possible.

The idea is to go the edge—of your comfort zone. You don't have to jump over, just tip-toe a little bit. If you don't feel comfortable doing something, then by all means, don't do it. However, if this is something you want to try but you feel weird talking like this in front of your significant other, fantasize about doing it first, or you can pretend he's your favorite fantasy guy, if you like. This might help you get over your initial inhibition.

You don't have to talk dirty all the way through sex. You can eventually just let your natural moans take over. All the "oohs" and "ahhs" that let him know he's doing a mighty fine job.

Be sure to let him know how much he pleased you afterwards.

YOU'VE BEEN A BAD, BAD GIRL

And you need to be punished.

Spanking someone else is nice, it's fun and cute but getting spanked is even better. However, does it mean there's something wrong with you? Probably not.

Spanking can make some people weak in the knees. "Come here, young lady, you're in big trouble!"

And that's usually all it takes.

Some people think people who do this sort of kinky stuff are freaky. Who are they to judge? It's not hurting anyone. Not much anyway.

The point of all this is to enhance your sex life, not really because you've been a bad girl and you need to be punished. Having a little spanking every so often can lead to good sex and it can bring a couple closer together. Sometimes it's necessary to dabble in fun and games where sex is concerned and to make it a bit naughty. If you never liven it up or try anything new, sex not only gets old, it gets stale and sometimes moldy. And spanking can be a good way to bring the new back to your sex life.

There is an art to spanking and, if you want to try it, it might be a little awkward to tell your man you want it. One way to approach it is when you're having doggie style sex, ask him to slap your butt. This will make you feel naughty and dirty and oh, so sexy. You might even want another slap on the butt. And if you want it, *you have to be punished for wanting it.* That's what makes spanking exciting—asking for punishment because you've been bad.

Nevertheless, be aware that you can put it into whatever context you want. It's your game. If you want a spanking because you're being punished or while you're being ridden, it doesn't matter. Make it work for you.

Get the idea?

If you ask him for a slap on the butt while you're having sex and he says, 'Huh?" just ignore it and get back on track. Afterwards, tell him what you wanted—a spanking. Ask him to spank you next time. If using the word "spanking" is uncomfortable, just ask him to slap you on the butt when you're doing it. This *really* heats things up. He might surprise you one day and pull you into his lap, push up your skirt and do it all on his own.

As he's spanking, he needs to know to use a flat hand on the buttocks, not on the hip or anywhere else, just on the buttocks. And he just needs to spank you, not hit you hard. Just a little slap. It can make an orgasm intensify. Or, it can excite a person enough to want to get down and dirty.

Also, many people like to use various things to get spanked with. If this isn't your cup of tea, then it isn't. No biggie. However, if you would like to incorporate various effects into your play, you can try a hairbrush, a riding crop or a whip. This might be too much for the novice and might be something you will have to work up to. (It *is* hard to ask someone to whip you with a riding crop!) Of course, you have to be with someone you totally trust that won't go over the edge and really beat you—that's *not* what you're after. All spanking, or whipping, does is to entice lovers into taking a little walk on the wild side. It's not about being beaten to a bloody pulp. A spanking game is just that—a game. It's a way to liven up your sex life, not bring about trust issues.

As I've said, spanking isn't for everyone. If you try it out and don't like it, just say so. But you might just uncover something that totally gets you in the mood for some wild sex. Remember to only travel within your comfort level. Never let anyone talk you into doing something that you don't want to do. You're in control, even if he's the one delivering the spanking. Or, if you have dominatrix tendencies, you might want to be in control yourself. Your call. Just play safe and don't get hurt.

ORAL SEX—HIS FAVORITE FANTASY OR YOUR WORST NIGHTMARE?

Oral sex. What can I say about oral sex that hasn't been said a million times? Not much. It is much better to receive than to give, perhaps?

Having good sex means loving everything about sex and that includes his penis. Yeah, it's time to think about giving your man a good blowjob. Once you can get over your reservations about putting "that thing" in your mouth, you can heat things up in the bedroom and probably ask for anything you want. All joking aside, giving him oral sex shouldn't be looked at as a dreaded task or something you only do on special occasions. It should be looked at as something you do because you love him and you want him to be satisfied. Men want orgasms like women want new shoes. The thought of oral sex for some men is enough to make them…well, come.

But most women just hate the very idea of giving a blowjob. It shouldn't be like that.

Truth is, if you're going to get it, you've got to give it. I've heard a lot of women complain about oral sex. In fact, I used to do this myself. Whenever my husband would want it, I'd wrinkle my nose and shake my head. There was something about it I just didn't like, though I couldn't put my finger on what it was exactly. I felt like it was demeaning and repulsive at the same time. It took me a few years to warm up to it, but once I did, I realized that it wasn't that big of deal and actually began to like doing it. All I had to do was ease into it, slow and steady. At first, I'd just kiss it, then I put it in my mouth, then I was able to give him a blowjob. After a while, I must say I had myself a very satisfied man.

There is an art to giving a good blowjob. But many women can't even work up enough nerve to even kiss it. Nevertheless, once you get over that initial trepidation, you're going to have a man who will worship you from here on out.

And isn't that what it's all about?

If you think about it, men do a lot when it comes to sex. They usually have to initiate it, then they have to get us all primed for it, then they have to hold out until we come. It seems like a lot of work, doesn't it? However, it's something they do willingly; they want to do it and do it all the time. If you think about it, women are more on the receiving end in this capacity than men are. Isn't it time for a little payback? It's it time to give your man what he really wants for Christmas? Give him the gift of head. But be warned, once you do it right, he will want it for all special, and not so special, occasions.

Keep in mind that if you cringe whenever you get near his penis or ask, "Do I *have* to?" he's going to feel like garbage. He wants you to like it and he wants you to do it only if you want to do it. Sure, he'll let you do it regardless, but if you actually enjoy doing it, you'll double his pleasure. This is one of the sexiest things a woman can do for her man. Getting into it is only icing on the cake.

Still feeling a tad apprehensive? Well, you might want to think about why you feel that way towards his little buddy. Sit back and think about it. I think it's that whole degradation thing. Many women feel degraded and put upon when they stick a penis in their mouths. It's like they think it's something bad that's being done to them, like a punishment of some sort. Like it's being foisted on them. They don't view it as doing something good for someone else but that's exactly what it is.

But some women aren't like that. Some women actually like oral sex and those women like it because they know they're in control. With oral sex, if you're sucking, you're in control. He isn't going to do anything until you say so. That is, unless he comes early.

Once you start doing it more often, oral sex might just be used a primer to get both of you going. And, once you learn to like, if not love, it, it will give you as much pleasure as it gives him. Really. Give it a try once and see where it leads to.

Before you begin, keep in mind that the most important thing to realize is that your mind should be concentrated on your blowjob task and not all over the place. Concentrate on his penis as if all you want to do is get him off. That should be your focus. Also, remember that the area around the tip of the penis, right around where the head starts, is the most sensitive and that's where you need to spend most of your time.

Now that you're ready to blow him like there's no tomorrow, do it. Get between his legs like a stripper and run your hands up and down his legs. Now, get your whole body into it, get into the groove. His hands will be all over you, of course, but that's okay. Just don't let them distract you from the task at hand. Start running your head up and down his body, taking your time. He should be about as hard a rock by now. Start to nibble on his penis through his pants, taking your time to really tease him. By now he's probably begging you to put it in your mouth. So, that's what you need to do. Unzip his pants and pull out his penis.

At this point, be gentle because you are going to give him a little hand job before you give him a little head. Lick the palms of your hands—for lube, that's all you need unless he requests some lotion—and grip his penis. Run your hands up and down it slowly, then with more vigor. Be sure to get a firm grip on his penis, but not too tightly! You might hurt him. Don't jerk. Handle it delicately but firmly. Use everything and concentrate on his penis. Stare up at him as you do this, make lots of eye contact.

Now, drop your mouth down onto it, taking the tip in your mouth and give a little but firm suck, using your tongue to lick as you do this. (This could take some practice to get it right, but at first just take it slow and concentrate on what you're doing.) Be warned that when you do this, he might come up off the bed. If he does, you're doing an excellent job.

Note: If you gag, you're not relaxing. *Relax.* If you are getting a little gag-reflex, then just relax your throat muscles and it should be fine. If you still feel a little gag, then you're just trying too hard to do it. Don't try too hard, just do it and soon it will come like second nature. Perhaps if you concentrate more on the tip instead of putting the entire penis in your mouth, you will enjoy it more.

Come back up for air and do a little dirty talk if you like. Talk to him like a porn star talks to her man. You can say stuff like, "You taste so good!" And then go right back down on it before he can answer. Make noises, lots of "Mmm!" and "Ahh!" Make noises like you are having the time of your life. Once you can lose your inhibition about doing it, you *can* start to enjoy it. Remember, the more you're into it, the more he'll be into it. Of course, he's into it from the get-go but knowing you like doing it might be enough to send him over the edge.

Just be gentle when you do it. Suck him like you're sucking your favorite sucker. I mean, not too hard and not too gentle. A balance must be maintained because if you suck too lightly, he won't get off and if you suck too hard, you might bruise him. Remember, a penis is a *very* sensitive thing. There's a reason why guys always cover themselves if they think their fella is in harm's way.

By now, if he's still holding it, let him get it out, otherwise, you risk giving him blue balls. And, by the way, don't neglect his balls. Give them a few gentle—very gentle!—squeezes and if you like, give them a few licks, taking them into your mouth and sucking gently. No Hoover action necessary.

However, you don't always have to bring him to orgasm when you give him a blowjob. You can do it for a little while, then climb aboard and have some hot sex. In fact, if you have an agreement that this is what you will do, it might take some of the apprehension away and help you to like it more. Also, it's good to practice a few times. Just do whatever makes you comfortable. Believe me, he won't complain as long as you're doing something.

If you want to spice it up, you can put his penis between your breasts just as he is about to come. This really turns a man on so much. There is something about seeing his semen on a woman's body that they love. Let's not try to analyze it and just accept this as fact.

A word on swallowing: If you don't want to, tell him so. But men love for you to swallow their semen. (A note: You should be aware that you can contract diseases from doing this, so it's important to be in a committed, monogamous relationship, preferably with someone who has been tested for sexually transmitted diseases. It's just safer that way, so always be careful.) They just do for some reason. It's like the ultimate compliment. Who really knows their reasoning?

But if you don't want to do it, pull back before he comes and let it splash on your breasts. Or you can take it in your mouth and let it slowly drip out of your mouth and down your chin. He will be out of his mind with lust for you.

A final word on deep-throating: You can try this move, but it is hard to do if you don't completely relax your throat muscles. You don't want to gag. If you want to do it, relax, then slowly move your mouth over the penis until you have it all in your mouth, then move back out slowly. Your mouth has to be open wide for this move. This might be a little advanced for the novice, but it's something that every man totally gets off on.

That's pretty much it. If you feel like you want to know what you're doing before you give your lover a blowjob, you can always buy a dildo to practice on. Once you conquer that, you can then conquer him.

TEACH HIM THE FINE ART OF CUNNILINGUS

Now it's *your* turn.

Giving head is nice but getting head is better. I don't think there's anything quite like the feeling of good cunnilingus. The most important thing, however, is to be receptive to it. If you allow yourself to enjoy getting it, then you're in for a very fun time. Not only is it fairly easy to orgasm during cunnilingus, it can also make sex better. If you're turned on while this is going on, think of how turned on you'll be during actual intercourse.

However, if the thought if cunnilingus doesn't give you a nice, funny feeling in your tummy, it might be because you haven't had it done to you right. A good man who knows how to give good head is indeed a hard man to find. That's why it might be suggested that you turn your man into that good man. He can learn and, better yet, you can teach him the fine art of cunnilingus.

If you find yourself with a man who is, to put it nicely, lacking in the cunnilingus department, why not tell him what you want? Or, you can just have him read this chapter to get an idea of what it's really all about. If cunnilingus is not done right, it can leave a girl feeling a little…left out. Most men do seem to have a lot of enthusiasm for this, that's not the problem. The main problem men seem to have is the fact that they do too much and don't concentrate enough. Knowing when to give more and when to pull back is what makes a good lover good. But, mostly, it's about doing what feels good for the woman at hand.

If you tell your man what you want, if you clue him in to your needs, he will most likely be happy to comply. If he does it right, you'll want it more and more.

However, it's just not up to him. There are many women out there who, for whatever reason, don't get into cunnilingus. Some women think that their vaginas are "weird looking" and sometimes "smelly." They just don't want anyone down there judging them. Of course, as we discussed in a previous chapter, there is nothing wrong with your vagina. It's the idea that something's wrong that's wrong. Once you can fix that, you can have some fun letting him go down on you.

Let's assume for arguments sake that you love it and he loves to do it. Even if you haven't gotten into it yet, you can get him to apply these techniques and soon you might just find yourself begging for it.

The most important thing for your man to do is to not just jump in by putting his hands down your pants. He needs to take his time to get you totally warmed up. He can do this by giving you a massage, running his hands all over your body, *then* he can put his hand between your legs and began to explore you with his fingers.

As you get turned-on, let him know you want more. Lie back and allow him to pull your clothes off, leaving your underwear on. He can then begin to nibble around your panties, which can be extremely sexy and a total turn-on. Just look down at him tugging at your panties and pushing them to the side to get at you. *Umm!* As he's doing this, you should begin to warm up and want more of what he can give you. Once you are sufficiently turned on, slide your legs open and let him get down to business.

Note: If you are not wet by this point, don't worry. Once he starts using his mouth and tongue on you, you will more than likely be ready for it. Just take your time and don't force anything. If, at any time, you want to call stop, you can. But if you hold out for a little while, you might find that you won't want to call stop.

What he is going to do is explore your vagina with his face and tongue, just like he did with his fingers. He should take his time to taste it, lick it, and kiss it. It might not be a bad idea to tease you a little, either. He can pull back from time to time so you will begin to want it more. Also, he can alternate from your vagina to your breasts and lips, taking his time to explore your most sensitive areas.

The most important thing to remember is that when he's going down on you, he needs to use a *relaxed* tongue. Never a pointy tongue! Never a tongue flick! That does nothing but make us wonder what he's doing. He should lick you as he would an ice cream cone. Cunnilingus, like intercourse, has a rhythm. You man needs to do it steady and not be all over the place while he's doing it. Remember, the key here is concentration.

To orgasm, you will need a bit of pressure on your clitoris. He can use his hand to do this or his mouth. All he has to do is suck at your clitoris, using a bit of pressure but not too much. The tongue shouldn't be hard, but firm and pliable. You might get a little noisy when he does this, so be warned. If he uses his hand, just have him place it flat against your clitoris and then rub against it. As you're doing this, pull him up to you and kiss him, or push his mouth down to your breasts.

In no time, you might be bucking up fro the bed and having a great orgasm. Coming this way is fantastic. All you can do is hang on for the ride.

If you would like to give while you get, you can try the 69, which is a personal favorite of mine. Everyone gets something out of it. Just have him lie down on the bed and climb on top of him, with his penis near your mouth. Now, go down on him and just wait. Soon, he'll be going down on you, too.

ANAL—IT'S EASY

Well, it's *kind* of easy. I have only done anal sex a few times and I must say…it's certainly different. It might be something you never want to try and if not, that's fine. For some, it's just not their bag. I just wanted to include this for the more adventurous of you. For me, it was something I wanted to try and see what I'd been missing out on. If it's not something you ever want to try, then don't try it. It's no big deal if you do or don't. As I've said, always do what *you're* most comfortable with and never force yourself to do anything you simply don't want to do.

Once you become less inhibited and your sex life gets better than good, this funny thing happens—you start wanting to experiment in all sorts of ways. Anal sex is normally a natural progression from "normal" sex and many couples try it at least once. Of course, you don't have to try it at all. For some, it's just not their thing. And, for others, they try it once and they're done. Some, too, like it just as much as regular sex.

If you do want to try it, know that being turned on is a must for anal sex. Most times, you will find yourself in the throes of passion and wanting a little more. Or, maybe, you might want to do it from the start. Whatever rocks your boat is fine, but just remember to proceed with caution.

To begin with, you may want him to just use his fingers, to see if you like it and can handle it. Just allow him to slide his hand between your butt cheeks and explore a little. He needs to be extra gentle when he slides a finger in. Easy does it. If you want more, you can have him insert a dildo in to see if you like it.

Many women want to stop there, as that's all the sensation they want. If you want to go all the way, you can climb up on all fours and prepare for a wild ride. The key with anal sex is that slow and steady wins the race. He has to enter you with care so he doesn't rip the skin. Also, lube is necessary. It is advisable to use a condom as anal sex can spread disease and infection. (As mentioned before, getting an AIDS test—and having him get one too—is always a good idea just to be safe.)

After he's in, let nature take its course. It might take a few tries to get it right. Afterwards, be sure to wash everything and don't go straight into regular sex—vaginal or oral sex—afterwards. Always keep it separate. You don't want to get any sort of infection.

That's about it. It's really not that big of a deal once you do it.

SHOW YOUR STUFF: EXHIBITIONISM

We all have an exhibitionist lurking beneath our surfaces. Most of the time, they stay hidden and only come out when we open ourselves up to the possibilities. Being an exhibitionist doesn't have to mean showing out at parties or becoming a stripper. It can mean, simply, just opening yourself up and exposing yourself to your lover.

Being nude around your significant other makes you more comfortable for sex. But you might have to start out just being nude around yourself. If you're not comfortable being nude alone, you will probably never be comfortable being nude around your lover. And if you're not that comfortable being nude, sex will probably not be that much fun.

I used to have this problem. Just after I got married, I could barely get undressed in front of my husband. I thought that he might look at me and judge, which, of course, he wouldn't have. If he ever caught a glimpse of naked skin, he wasn't thinking about judging me, he was thinking about having a naked woman in close proximity.

Most men are like this. They really don't judge our fat rolls or cellulite and, truth be told, they never even notice them unless we point them out to them. (For some reason, we always do that, too. Maybe we *want* to be judged.)

But, for me, I didn't always want to be that type of person who ran for cover right after sex or getting out of the bathtub. I wanted to be able to walk around naked and feel comfortable doing it. One day, I found myself alone at home and I thought, "Why don't I try it? Why don't I get naked and see how it feels?" and that's what I did. (If you have children, why not get a sitter and do this?)

Soon, being naked around the house was cool with me. I didn't mind walking around without clothes on. I also became aware that I had stopped asking my husband if I was "fat" and stopped pointing out my "faults." Mostly, I just flaunted around in front of him from time to time, to let him know what he has. (And he loves it.)

This wasn't enough, though. I wanted to see how far I could push it. One vacation, we found ourselves near a nude beach and, to make a long story short, I dared myself to go to it. Yeah, that's right, I went to a nude beach and it was one of the most liberating experiences of my life.

Of course, it was also the most nerve-wracking thing I'd ever done. But, thinking back on it, going there probably saved me ten years of therapy. And you know why? Because it really helped me to get over a lot of my inhibitions. In fact, it kind of forced the inhibition out of me. After I got over the initial shock of being nude, I began to relax and that meant I could relax doing everything, especially sex. And the main reason was because I realized that being naked in front of other people wasn't that big of a deal. And, after I did it, I realized something else. My body was just a body out among all these other nude bodies. Sure, some of the men looked at me and I even looked at some of them. What's the big deal?

The funny thing was that after a few minutes, I kind of forgot that I didn't have any clothes on. And, since every one else was nude, the fact that I was nude didn't make me stand out. In fact, I would have been more uncomfortable if I had been wearing clothes. It was odd that I'd made this big thing out of it in my mind but the actual doing was less nerve-racking than the thinking about doing.

What spurred me to try it? Well, first of all, I had a lot of these dreams about being nude in public. So, obviously, I had an issue with it and I've found the best way to overcome issues is to deal with them head-on. Also, I knew that doing something that daring would help me to get over other hang-ups and free myself of a lot of inhibition. And it has. It was a big step for me but after I did it, I realized how silly and stupid I was about the whole thing.

Nothing held me back more than my fear of the unknown. The fear is what made me think of sex in a "bad" way. It was the fear that was embedded in me that was wrong, not the real feelings of exposure.

Now, even though I rarely do it, I can go to a nude beach and strip off without a problem. I'm not a nudist or anything, but it's knowing that I can do it, if I like, that's important. I do love to sunbathe nude; there is nothing like it in the world. I don't care if people are looking at me in a sexual way anymore. I know they sometimes do and, as humans, we do that with one another. It's natural. I didn't feel like a piece of meat, either.

Now, now, I am not saying that you have to do this. *No, I'm not.* I am not the boss of you. But if it's something you want to do and you have someone you trust—you have to have someone you trust to go with you—why not? It's always your choice to do with your body what you like. No one else should ever convince you to do it if you don't want to do it. No one convinced me. It was my idea from the get-go. My husband almost fell out of his chair when I first approached him with the idea and he agreed to it because I wanted to do it.

The point of all this is to show you that nudity—and exposure—is not that big of a deal. There is nothing wrong with it! You shouldn't be afraid to show yourself to anyone, but especially not to your lover. You shouldn't be afraid to show it off to yourself. No one really cares, you know? No one cares whether you do it or not. And if it's something you want to do, you should be able to do it regardless.

Show it all off to your lover and let him look. Know that he wants to touch you and let him do it. Open yourself up to him and let him see the real you, every single inch of the real you. I'll bet he'll like what he sees.

OBJECTIFY YOURSELF!

My husband thinks I am a smart, intelligent person. But he still sees me as a woman and that means, when he looks at me, he sees me as a sexual creature. And I wouldn't have it any other way.

The thing that keeps most of us from having great sex is our inability to see ourselves as sexual beings. We can't "objectify" ourselves—what would the feminists think? But the fact is that no matter how far we go, we can never lose site of what makes us innately human and what makes us human is the simple fact that we are sexual beings.

Sex is a gift that we give one another. It's something that is shared between lovers. Is there anything in the world like sex? Why would anyone want to do anything besides have sex, especially when it's so hot and intense?

And the thing is, you don't have to have the perfect setting to have good sex. You can do it on top of the washing machine with most of your clothes still on. In fact, having a few articles that he can push to the side—like your bra—on while you're doing it is such a turn on. Just stare down at him while he's devouring your breast. *Uph!* Now that's what I'm talking about. Being that turned on means being alive and feeling alive is the best feeling on earth.

So, I say, be alive and if that entails objectifying yourself then that's what it entails. By this I mean, buy that slutty outfit and model it for him. Feel like a sex object from time to time and be proud to feel that way. This means you are a total woman! It doesn't mean you're a whore or any other bad name you might call a woman who does this kind of thing.

It is our so-human attributes that cause people to get weird. Sexual desire is a huge part of being a human, but, somehow, some of us get the idea that it's uncouth. We're afraid of our desires because someone might think badly of us. What they don't know can't hurt them. So what if you're a schoolteacher during the day? At night, you can be his slut or his mistress or his sex object. At night, you can turn into a wild woman, a woman who loves sex and gets off because she can, because she wants to. You don't have to have any other reason to do it other than the fact that you want to.

The greatest hindrance to a great sex life isn't what's going on between your legs but between your ears. Your brain might be keeping you from having mind-blowing sex. Most of the time, it's getting out of the habit of sex that leads to the lack of sex. So, get back into the habit, objectify yourself and let him take part. For this time, during this part of the day, you two can see each other as you saw each other the first time you felt that spark—like sexual beings. And all you have to do is start making the effort.

Sure, there are a lot of things that need to get done during the day and at night you might be too tired. I say, try it first thing in the morning; even take a shower together if you want to. Maybe lie in bed and cuddle before the busy day starts. Yes, we do live in a hectic environment but what's the use if there's no fun involved and no sex to be had? We all need something to look forward to, even if it's just a little time with our vibrators or our significant others. If we never view ourselves as needing sex, the need will go away. And that is a terrible loss.

So, turn on the sexual being and let the objectification begin. Do this by becoming aware that you are a woman with needs that deserve to be met. Your lover will probably totally agree.

HE'S YOURS

Your man. If you try hard enough, you will find something wrong with him. He may be one of those men who always leaves the toilet seat up. He may have forgotten your birthday last year. Or, he may watch too much football. Sure, all of these things are annoying, but, really, in the greater scheme of things, they're not even blips on the radar.

So, I say, don't be like that. Don't dog your man for spending too much time in his lazy-boy. He works hard, right? He deserves a beer. And he deserves to be told he's good from time to time.

Men need validation as much as women. It's just that we don't normally give it to them. Men have to be strong and they can't do the things women do—like crying or shopping—or someone might make fun of them. They have to keep the proverbial stiff upper lip.

Why not tell him how good he is from time to time? Look at him and find something good. Maybe he's big and strong. Maybe he makes lots of money. Maybe he's a good cook. Maybe he's going to get the band back together and you can be his groupie. Find something about your man that you love and then embellish on that until you love all of him, even his faults.

When it's all said and done, touch him. Go on now, don't be shy. Touch him. Feel his biceps and how strong they are. Run your hand along his chin and feel the whiskers. Look into his eyes and notice what color they are and how handsome he looks. Notice how he's looking at you and feel a surge of power from it. He's *yours*, he's your man. You wouldn't have it any other way, would you?

FALL IN LOVE ALL OVER AGAIN

Once we get into "serious" relationships, we stop becoming a mystery to each other. I say, start it up again. Become a mystery like you used to be and fall in love all over again. Putting the spark back into your relationship entails things just like this. It entails giving longing looks and secret smiles shared between the two of you, two lovers.

It might be good to know that as far as sex goes, men don't expect or, really, need that much to get going. I once asked a good male friend of mine, "What does a woman have to do to turn you on?"

He said, "Show up."

But really. Is there any more to it than that? Yeah, there is, but not much. A woman who pleases her man in the bedroom is not only sexually satisfied and empowered, but she has him right where she wants him. He isn't going to go anywhere to find something else if he's being pleased and he's going to do whatever it takes to please.

Re-teach each other how to please. Do things together that you used to enjoy. Make a point to spend time together every day, even if it's just for a few minutes. Doing this will bring you closer together and that will lead to good sex.

The most important thing you can do for your man is to let him know that you want him. Believe me, this is enough for your man. As long as he knows you want to get busy with him, he's fine. Just ask him.

Another thing, treat him special from time to time. Men act like they don't care for that candles and wine sort of stuff, but they do. Who doesn't like to be treated special? Be good to him and he'll be better to you. Take the time to be special for one another. Like I said, fall in love again and stop treating each other like a roommate. Stop yelling about the dishes and the laundry and start supporting each other. It's not that hard to do this and once you start, life will get better.

Once in a while, tell each other what you find special about the other. And do something fun and spontaneous.

Here are a few fun things to do together:
- Go outside at night. Get a blanket and make love under the stars.
- Go have your pictures taken together. Buy an 8x10 and frame it and put it up with all your other artwork.
- Practice hearing each other's fantasies and your reactions.
- Cook in a meal together, just the two of you. Do not order in food of any kind. And, if you have kids, send them to grandma's.
- Read erotica to each other.

Things to do and for each other:
- Slaps on the ass—it's playful!
- Make a point to ask each other how your day was.
- Listen.
- Turn off the TV while talking or having sex because it's distracting.
- Give each other backrubs.
- Call each other up at work during the middle of the day and ask, "What are you doing?"

- Meet at least once a week for lunch, if possible, or for dinner. *Just the two of you.*
- Take a weekend away together at least once a year.
- Plan a grown-up vacation to Vegas. Stay in a suite and feel like a movie star.
- Buy a good bottle of wine and open it after the kids have gone to bed.
- Move the TV out of the bedroom.
- Do special things for each other like buying a nice, inexpensive gift of Magic Eight Ball or something as silly.
- Get the old CDs out that you used to make love to and listen to them together, recalling those wild times. (Barry White is always a favorite.)
- Do things "just because I love you."
- Never forget why you got together—because you had a spark and fell in love. Remind each other of these things and feel blessed.
- Fall in love all over again and do this by treating each other like lovers instead of roommates.

BECOMING SEXUALLY SATISFIED

A sexually satisfied woman is a happy, happy woman. The best thing about this is that we can give it to ourselves. We can all have a great, uninhibited sex lives and all we have to do is take a few steps here and there in order for it to happen.

Here is a short list of the things I've talked about in this book in order to have a good sex life. It's about being less inhibited and more open to the possibilities.

How to become less inhibited and have a good sex life:
- Get rid of sexual baggage.
- Recognize your inner slut.
- Work through the issues with your mom.
- Recognize repression and deal with the underlying issues with it.
- Forgive yourself for past mistakes.
- Form an open-line of communication with your lover/husband, etc…
- Relinquish control in the bedroom to your man.
- Sometimes, have your man relinquish control to you.
- Explore your innermost fantasies.
- Explore your body, including your vagina.
- Learn what turns you on by masturbation.
- Wear slutty/sexy clothes whenever you want, but especially for your man.

- Accept your man's porn stash and the fact that he spanks the monkey. He's a man, and men do these things.
- Give yourself over to a good kiss.
- Say "I love you" and mean it.
- Explore dirty talk, spanking or anything else you like.
- Let him worship your body through foreplay.
- Give him what he wants from time to time, including doggie style and oral sex.
- Let him—or teach him—how to give you good head.
- Show your stuff through exhibitionism—at least to your man.
- Realize that it's not what's between your legs that keeps you from having good sex, but what's in your head.
- Love all of your lover, even his flaws.
- Love all of yourself, even your flaws.

Once you can overcome some of your obstacles to getting your sex life back on track, there's going to be no stopping you. Claim that sexual being inside of you and let her out. One way to do this is to get rid of the excuses of *what has to happen before you'll have good sex.*

What I think has to happen before I have good sex, a.k.a. my excuses:
- I have my baby.
- My baby gets older.
- My career dies down.
- I get a better job.
- I get better lingerie.
- I lose some weight.
- When I'm not so busy.

- Anything else you can think of to distract you from getting busy.

It's time to get over all that. Sex is good and, if it's what you want, it's never a mistake. Sex is a stress reliever; it brings on good feelings, and is an endorphin releaser. I could go on and on advocating sex. Pretty soon, you might do this as well.

Remember, if it feels good, it is good. Good sex gives you confidence. It makes you smile during the day to think about what you did last night. Isn't it time to get that good feeling back?

IN THE END, IT'S WHAT YOU DO TOGETHER THAT COUNTS

If you don't put anything into your relationship, how can you expect to get anything out of it? It is a two-way street. Take time with your lover. If all you can get is a few minutes in the morning or at night, then get it. Sit down and talk about your day, your fears, things that are bothering you. Don't make this entire discussion about the bills or kids or an old grudge, try to talk about what's going on inside you.

Now, after you've re-familiarized yourself with your lover, do something dramatic and fun. Make a date.

When you were dating, he always asked you out, right? Make him do it again. Make a date and come hell or high water, keep it. Agree to meet somewhere and go out. At least once a year, go away for an entire weekend *alone.* Even if it's just to your local hotel. Even if you just sit and watch TV the entire time. Take a bathing suit and splash around the pool.

You can do all the things you always hear about doing. Like going to the park and holding hands while sitting on a bench. Like sneaking behind a tree for a little make-out session. Like meeting each other in a bar and sitting a few seats away from each other and pretending to be strangers. These things really do work. Take a Friday night out alone. If you have kids, get a sitter or send them to grandma's.

Someone once told me, "If I hadn't taken time away from my kids, my husband and I would have nothing to talk about now. In fact, we wouldn't really know each other."

This is because people do change. You're always changing, as is your significant other. Change is good, it's necessary. But you both need to keep abreast of it.

What you need to have a great sex life:
- A willing partner that you trust.
- A place or room in which to do it.

That's all. You don't need wine. You don't need roses. You just need someone to get down and dirty with. Someone you trust. Someone that you're attracted to. And someone you love.

I don't think that sexual problems exist because someone needs lube or a new position. I think sexual problems exist because we were taught that sex is bad and that it is not good for us to enjoy it. Now it's time to un-teach ourselves. It's time to get on to the best thing in life and enjoy it for what it is.

We all have our problems and we all have things about ourselves that we would like to change for the better. But in the end, it's important not to concentrate on that too much, lest it drive you crazy. It's best to concentrate on what you can do not only to improve your sex life but to improve your well-being. But I think once you take care of the sex part, all the repression and shame will inevitably take care of itself. That's what happened to me and hopefully, that's what can happen for you, if you so desire.

Make your life a little more exciting. All work and no play makes everyone dull. Do this by turning off the TV from time to time and talking about your ideal fantasy. This will take time to build up to, so start out slow and don't be judgmental if his fantasy is the "school girl." Likewise, he shouldn't be upset if your fantasy is "a dark stranger in an elevator." Even so, it's just a fantasy! As you talk, really listen to each other and if something sexy comes out of it, even if it's just a little kiss, then, hey, life's getting better.

Keep in mind that one of the most inhibiting things is not being able to voice your needs and desires. That's why having a partner you totally trust is so important. That's what you're trying to build up to. Opening up about what you'd like is hard, I'll grant you that. It took me years to tell my man about my desires. Having been raised in a strict background didn't help matters, but once I was able to open up, the floodgates just opened. Now I confide in him most of my needs and even some fantasies. I keep some to myself, just because I just like to keep some things to myself. Besides, he doesn't need to know *every*thing.

Laugh more together. Laughing together is about as good an aphrodisiac as any out there. Laughing together means you like each other. That's a good thing.

Let all expectations go out the window. By that I mean, don't expect either party to do anything more than they're willing. Never expect to "get laid" and never "get laid" if you don't feel like it. Do what you feel like doing. Never feel pressure to do it and, if you do, sit down and talk about it. Sometimes, you're just not in the mood. It's as simple as that. But when you are in the mood, go for it and go for it with gusto. The next day you might just think about what you did the previous night and blush. It was that good, wasn't it?

Good sex doesn't take that much effort. As long as you're willing to put a little in, you're sure to get a lot out of it.

And that's really all there is to good sex.